THE DAYTON ANTHOLOGY

MORE CITY ANTHOLOGIES FROM BELT

The Louisville Anthology

The Gary Anthology

Car Bombs to Cookie Tables: The Youngstown Anthology, Second Edition

The Columbus Anthology

The St. Louis Anthology

Under Purple Skies: The Minneapolis Anthology

The Milwaukee Anthology

Rust Belt Chicago: An Anthology

Grand Rapids Grassroots: An Anthology

Happy Anyway: A Flint Anthology

The Akron Anthology

Right Here, Right Now: The Buffalo Anthology

The Cleveland Anthology, Second Edition

The Pittsburgh Anthology

A Detroit Anthology

The Cincinnati Anthology

THE DAYTON ANTHOLOGY

EDITED BY SHANNON SHELTON MILLER

Belt Publishing

First Edition 2020
ISBN: 978-1-948742-80-1

Belt Publishing
5322 Fleet Avenue, Cleveland, OH 44105
www.beltpublishing.com

Book design by Meredith Pangrace
Cover by David Wilson

CONTENTS

CONTENTS

2019

Introduction

I don't remember when I first learned of the Wright brothers, but it was likely sometime in elementary school, either in a social studies class or on a field trip where they were mentioned among other American greats. As the generalized story went, the brothers were the first to achieve powered flight in 1903 when they kept their flying machine aloft on a windy December day in Kitty Hawk, North Carolina, launching the modern age of aviation. We learned they owned a bicycle shop, and that they hailed from Dayton, Ohio.

The Dayton part was an afterthought in my young mind, but I remembered that fact when I first came to Dayton to attend a summer camp at Wright State University, of all places. More than a decade later, I returned as a sports writer covering the NCAA men's basketball tournament at the University of Dayton, a school with "Flyers" as its nickname.

When I began spending more time in Dayton in 2009 before moving the following year, I recognized how much the Wright brothers were a part of what made Dayton, *Dayton*, and why the city continued to embrace their story more than a century later. Here were two local boys without high school diplomas who used their curiosity and keen interest in engineering—along with the lessons learned about balance from building bicycles—to surpass more heralded and funded competitors in the international race to achieve flight.

Dayton is too often an afterthought among Ohio cities, with the "three Cs" of Columbus, Cincinnati, and Cleveland casting an oversized shadow over this mid-sized region in the southwestern part of the state. But Dayton never counts itself out. This is a city of invention and creativity, a place where innovators can rub shoulders with others with great ideas. It's where a young African-American poet, Paul Laurence Dunbar, could present his early works to the world thanks to the printing company owned by his high school friend, Orville Wright, and his brother Wilbur. It's where John H. Patterson's cash register, Charles Kettering's self-starting engine, and the Wright brothers' flying machines emerged within a twenty-year period in the early 1900s, making Dayton the Silicon Valley of its day. America thrived on Daytonian ingenuity.

While there is no singular Dayton story and *A Dayton Anthology* should not be read as the definitive text of the region, one can get a sense of the city's essence through the common themes that bind this diverse collection of stories. In the first section, simply titled "Flight," you'll read tributes to the Wright brothers and Dunbar, along with authors' reflections on their own brushes with Dayton's aviation history. We then move to "Dayton Stories," which shares lesser-known tales of Dayton history, both public and personal. Come along and discover how a funk music movement grew from West Dayton and its public school music programs by following that same path of innovation and collaboration that put Dayton's local talent against the best in the world—with the Daytonians often coming out on top.

Some of us were born in Dayton, while some arrived by choice. Others found ourselves here due to circumstances outside our control, but made a choice to remain. "Love Letters" tells those stories of sorrow, triumph, and acceptance of finding home.

When I launched the first call for submissions for *A Dayton Anthology* in July 2019, Dayton had just endured a harrowing Memorial Day weekend that started with a Ku Klux Klan rally that proved to be more of a public nuisance than the violent clash we feared. Nature, however, proved to be a stronger foe. As we prepared to conclude that holiday weekend thankful that the KKK threat had passed, seventeen tornadoes hit the region late that Monday night, decimating neighborhoods and businesses—many of which still were recovering a year later.

But nothing prepared us for August 4.

In response to tragedy, writers feel even more compelled to share their words. A significant number of submissions I received addressed the mass shooting in the Oregon District in the early hours of that Sunday morning in August, and the nine innocent lives lost. The anthology concludes with "2019," a section devoted to the ways we responded to the tragedies of one of Dayton's most trying years.

The process of creating this anthology has encompassed some of the most pivotal moments in recent years for our city, our nation and our world. As I write this foreword in 2020 in the midst of a global pandemic and ongoing protests for social and racial justice, I take note of how Dayton has attempted to respond to its citizens' cries in a year we hoped would be a respite from the pain of 2019.

Our character won't let us succumb, and if our history is any indication, Daytonian innovation will emerge again to help us thrive. Like the Wright brothers, we can't help but soar.

—*Shannon Shelton Miller*

A Toast to Dayton

PAUL LAURENCE DUNBAR

Love of home, sublimest passion
That the human heart can know!
Changeless still, though fate and fashion
Rise and fall and ebb and flow,
To the glory of our nation,
To the welfare of our state,
Let us all with veneration
Every effort consecrate.
And our city, shall we fail her?
Or desert her gracious cause?
Nay—with loyalty we hail her
And revere her righteous laws.
She shall ever claim our duty,
For she shines—the brightest gem
That has ever decked with beauty
Dear Ohio's diadem.

Published in Selected Poems *(1917)*

A Love Letter to Dayton

AMANDA DEE

"I think it's because one has no words that one writes," Sandra Cisneros wrote, and I believe this is why I have been unable to do much besides write about Dayton since the morning of August 4, when nine people were killed and 27 others were injured, outside Ned Peppers bar by a man armed with a semiautomatic weapon. My heart is broken. What else is left to say? What else must be said for us to put an end to this bloodshed? I have no words, so I am writing.

Dayton was my home for five and a half years. I attended the University of Dayton, and stayed behind, after graduation, as most of my classmates and friends fled to the coasts or larger cities (as I would later do myself). When I became editor-in-chief of the city's alt weekly, *Dayton City Paper*, it became my job to know Dayton intimately. Every week, I planned and edited dining reviews, music previews, art features, opinion columns. I helped cover the stores, restaurants, and bars in the Oregon District.

On weekends, I went to those stores, restaurants, and bars. I saw all the Oscar-nominated shorts at The Neon. I sipped whiskey like I was in a speakeasy at Century Bar. I still wear my Omega Records T-shirt almost every other week. I swung on the giant swings outside of Ned Pep's, as my friends Allison and Tinkle like to call it. In courting the city, I fell in love with it.

This city that wants for naught, that has innovated from nothing and welcomed all (it was the first "Certified Welcoming" city for immigrants in the U.S.)—despite being abandoned time and time again by those who had once invigorated it; this Rust Belt sequel to Detroit; this city, broken as it has been, loves fiercely back.

In my years covering Dayton, I saw firsthand one of the community's central contradictions: so much of the city is full of life, while some of it is, simply, empty, never re-filled after the exodus of manufacturing jobs that began in the 1970s. Dayton has also struggled to address its vast expanse of food deserts, ranking as one of the worst metropolitan areas in the country for food hardship. Then, hit hard and fast by overdoses, Dayton became a poster city for discussions of the opioid crisis in national news outlets. In 2017, the influx of bodies was so overwhelming, the county morgue had to outsource their handling to local funeral homes.

That same year, I left the paper and the city to move to Chicago, becoming another statistic in the decades-long population decline of Dayton. The *City Paper*, like many alt weeklies, would shut down within a year for financial reasons, silencing one of the loudest (and weirdest) voices that celebrated the city. Then in May, thirteen tornadoes tore through the region, taking more homes from the area, including the home of one of my friends, a former *City Paper* writer, whose family huddled, screaming, inside the house, while their roof flew away, along with the artifacts they had collected from their life.

You will hear many refer to the grit of Dayton, including the mayor and former residents. I have witnessed this side of Dayton, too. My friend, the writer, and his family raised enough money through community support to leave the motel they were living in for a mobile home. When the financial sustainability of the city's three main performing arts organizations was at risk, the Dayton Performing Arts Alliance formed in 2012, merging the symphony orchestra, ballet, and opera under the roof of one organization in what may be the first project of its kind in the U.S. In response to more grocery store closings in the area, more grassroots initiatives are on the rise. In one year, Dayton reduced opioid overdoses by nearly fifty percent, and other cities around the country are now looking to it to model solutions.

I've been thinking about another Sandra Cisneros quote these last few days, this one about death. "There is no getting over death," she writes, "only learning to travel alongside it." The only thing I have left to say is Thank you, Dayton. I love you, with my whole broken heart. You have taught me how to fight for the places and people I love, and to rally when life takes or is taken from us. As you travel alongside what has happened, I know this is what you will do again now.

This essay was previously published in Belt Magazine.

FLIGHT

Thinking About Flight

HERBERT WOODWARD MARTIN

Those two Wright brothers were more like Icarus than we care to believe. We like to think the best of our past, remembering only with affection, Icarus, who first achieved flight, and in the process, forgot the rest of his contenders. It has never mattered who takes second or third place since History is only going to remember the face of him or her who took first and stood in the center of the photograph. Most likely the other achievers will be slightly out of focus with no identifying name. History has only to do with those individuals who dare to dare and fly too high or too close to the edge of the known universe. We, who are survivors of Icarus, take our warnings seriously. Whoever takes the screws and bolts of his father's imagination, like Mozart or to a lesser degree the Bach sons can easily take wind and space and hold them in an affectionate embrace longer than a quarter of an hour which is a test of our faulty human memories.

Happiness

MARY COMBS

Restless for challenge in young manhood,
They chose the last frontier on earth,
Becoming monks in an Aeronautical Order.

Nimble cyclists, they knew that adjustment,
Not fixed stability was the secret to control.
Brilliant engineers, they saw that control
Was the secret of flight.

Two great minds focused through a single lens,
They considered the death of Lilienthal and failure of Langley,
Testing their theories in the heated laboratories of each other's brains

At work in blue and white striped aprons
Over shirts with high, stiff collars
Tucked into trousers with legs round as stovepipes,
They built bicycles, kites,
And the Kittyhawk Flyer.

Finally, tented on the moaning sands of the Outer Banks,
Orville strummed his mandolin and,
Wilbur pondered angles of incidence,
While they waited for daylight when the world would change.

Inspired by Orville Wright's quote: "Wilbur and I could hardly wait for the morning to come to get at something that interested us. That's happiness."

Church of the Overcast

ASHLEY STIMPSON

There is that famous photo of the horses swimming down Fourth Street.

After the flood, city leaders hung a banner from the courthouse. *Remember the promises you made in the attic.* Staggered Daytonians, their carpets still sodden with three rivers of water, raised enough money to build five dams.

I hung the photo of the horses above Southern mantels, in the entryway of a home on the edge of the Great Plains. I wanted people to see them—the desperate, frenzied horses—and know where I had come from. A place of great misery, a place of great resilience.

A kid from our second-grade class returned from Disney World and reported that an animatronic Thomas Edison spoke of "two brothers in North Carolina, working on some kind of flying contraption." That afternoon we transcribed letters of complaint from the blackboard, *To whom it may concern.*

A Midwestern childhood is like a religion. Some people remain. Some convert to other regional ideologies. Some leave the faith but never really join another; they arrange Midwestern iconography in prominent places around their homes. Everything they write is secretly about the cornfields that grow wild and un-reaped inside their chests.

Before large altars of stone, the Pinnacles of the Great Miami—now buried beneath landfill—two brothers watched turkey vultures bank and glide, turn and float, using only the tips of their sun-gilded feathers.

I once fell in love with a man who was far away. I walked down to the same river and took a picture of the skyline, slashed through with railroads and windows glistening like fresh rain. I emailed it to him. In the subject line I wrote: *This is me.*

Out of frame: two bronze brothers made vulture wings with their fingers.

―――――――――

The windows belong to John Patterson. The daylight factories. The chairs with back support. The park system. And then. Boats for the flood. Beds for the displaced. Some other kind of corporate welfare.

―――――――――

The railroad tracks are mine. Railroad tracks to nowhere, to all-night burger joints in the bad part of town. We grew up bored as hell on the shoulders of holy men, in the shadows of their hollowed-out relics. We slept in basements, stacked up like cordwood. We passed around weed in a pencil box. We took surreptitious sips of liquor from dining-room hutches. We had no idea what to do with the weed.

We found the limits of our inherited faith, and we leaned up against them. We found holes in fences and when we couldn't, we climbed up and over them; someone always ripped their jeans.

―――――――――

The DP&L Longworth Steam Plant, at the corner of Perry and Eaker Streets, was built like a church, a gothic leviathan. We prowled its catwalks, flipped the switches of its neutered motherboards. We sat nestled in its turrets, above Norman windows crowned in stone crosses. There's no reason to build a steam plant like a shrine; there's no reason not to.

When friends from college came to visit, I led them inside the shuttered plant. As if to say: *this is me.*

―――――――――

I was born 100 years after John Patterson bought the patent for a money-counting machine. I was born three blocks away from his company's headquarters, where my grandfather reported to a desk every day for three decades. I skipped school and smoked cigarettes at Woodland Cemetery, Patterson's body nearby; Kettering, Huffman, the Wrights looking on.

Woodland's highest point is Dayton's highest point, and there the trees part and the city poses in the near distance, humble as a paperweight. In 1913, they gathered in this place to look out over the Miami River Valley and search for a hint of their eaves, a weathervane, the nerve to keep going.

More than a century later the ground is still worn down by a thousand shuffling pilgrims, people like me, who came to worship and to wonder when I might be released.

Not knowing then that the city would release me like a mother.

An old lard can was placed under the banner. The promises in the attic came in the form of pennies, nickels, dimes. Tithes that built the dams, to keep my hometown dry.

The promises we make in the attic are not contracts. They are the same promises we make when a lover threatens to leave, or we travel to see a dying relative. We will call more, we will send money. We will love more, we will love better. Even NCR left eventually.

A promise made in fear or guilt is not a promise at all. It is a prayer. And you can't hold people's prayers against them. The five dams that tamed three rivers were built by something much bigger than obligation. They were built by a cabal: the church of the overcast.

A Midwestern childhood is like a religion. Some leave but never lapse. Everything they write is a secret missive, to whom it may concern—

My name is Ashley and I am thirty-five years old. I grew up in a tidy plat of tired houses behind Bob's Food Warehouse on Woodman Drive. Despite what you have read on southern license plates, Dayton, Ohio, is the birthplace of aviation, of the Wright brothers. It is the birthplace of *my* brothers. It is the birthplace of boredom and big windows and lard cans full of coins.

Where the winter sky hangs so low you can catch it on your tongue like snowflakes. Where I dreamed the dreams of leaving and the only promise I ever made was to never come back.

Where turkey vultures soar like eagles and the horses swim all the way to Keowee Street.

At Least One Wilbear Wright Has a Home—A Trip Down Dayton's Aviation Trail

C.L. SIMONSON

Born and raised in the Dayton area, I gained an appreciation for aviation history at an early age, well before I knew that its path practically ran through my backyard.

Aviation Trail, Inc. was founded in 1981. It's a not-for-profit run by volunteers that oversees eighteen aviation-related sites around the Miami Valley, eleven of which are directly in Dayton. If you take their map and visit at least seven sites by obtaining stamps, you'll then receive an aviator bear affectionately named "Wilbear Wright" at the last required stop—the Dayton Aviation Heritage National Historical Park.

I learned of the trail and decided to give it a whirl in 2016 when I held summer jobs at the National Museum of the United States Air Force (where the National Aviation Hall of Fame is also located) and Carillon Historical Park (which houses the 1905 Wright Flyer III in the John W. Berry Sr. Wright Brothers Aviation Center), both prominent stops on the trail.

I figured if getting those first few stamps out of the way was *that* easy, how hard would it be to get the rest? Well …

———

After that summer, I began a new adventure that took me away from my mission, but a key event two years later would inspire me to dig my map back out and visit, at the very least, the local sites on the trail.

On May 17, 2018, when the Museum of the United States Air Force unveiled the restored, iconic World War II plane, the B-17F Memphis Belle, I was determined to see it.

Suspended from the roof of the hangar, she's a beauty to behold in person. When gazing up at the turret and seeing just how *small* a space it is … I definitely gained an appreciation for the men who had the job of the ball turret gunner during World War II.

The museum's World War II gallery also has a display dedicated to the Doolittle Raiders, and other popular planes on display include the Strawberry Bitch and the famous Bockscar (the plane that dropped the second atomic bomb they called "Little Boy").

A few weeks after seeing the Memphis Belle, between two sunny, beautiful June afternoons, I finally visited enough sites on the trail to earn my Wilbear. It wasn't really about getting Wilbear, though; never mind how cute the little fella is. On my journey of the Aviation Trail, I was discovering so much more, and I didn't even know it.

On the map, two sites are labeled the Dayton Aviation Heritage National Historical Park and Huffman Prairie Flying Field Interpretive Center. Driving up a steep hill to the park, you'll see a huge memorial dedicated to the Wright brothers, which stands tall and proud.

While you'll get your stamp for the Huffman Prairie Flying Field at the memorial site, the prairie itself is down the road. It's a beautiful, peaceful area of land where the Wright brothers built hangars to keep equipment and supplies and to store their prototypes and such.

The Wright State University Special Collections and Archives Paul Laurence Dunbar Library is just down the road. It's a nifty little room that houses books that the Wright brothers owned, medals they received for their aviation feats, and neat sculptures.

The next afternoon I went to the Historic Woodland Cemetery and Arboretum. Dayton's most notable are buried there, including, of course, the Wright brothers. There's a beautiful gazebo area from which you can get the best view ever of the downtown Dayton skyline.

I concluded my journey at the last site of the trail at the Dayton Aviation Heritage National Historical Park (which includes stamps for the Wright-Dunbar Interpretive Center and the Wright Cycle Company, as well as the Aviation Trail, Inc. Visitor Center and Parachute Museum). I proudly handed the attendant my stamped brochure, and he happily handed me Wilbear.

What's neat about the location of this site is that it's literally where the Wright brothers lived and worked back in the day, as their bicycle shop still remains. Yup, before they discovered the gift of flight, they worked there. Before that though, they ran a successful print shop. Part of Williams Street is still brick and renovated pastel-colored houses line the street, but the neighborhood still captures that early 1900s feel. Paul Laurence Dunbar's home is a few blocks away (and that's a stop on the trail too).

After receiving Wilbear, I felt a sense of accomplishment, but my journey wasn't quite over. On my drive home, I made a pit stop at The Barrel House. As I sipped a light pilsner, chilled, and looked at Wilbear, I thought about all the other Wilbears sitting on the shelf back at the heritage park and about who they'd all go home with.

I also got to thinking about all the great things our wonderful Gem City has to offer. It always amazes me when people say there isn't much to do here. We need to put our cell phones down, get off Facebook, step away from Netflix, and pull back the curtain a bit. Get out. Explore. Investigate. Educate ourselves.

Sure, all towns have a story, a history—but part of our story is that the Wright brothers lived here, worked here, built here.

Like the Wright brothers, Dayton and her inhabitants are far more resilient than the world might know. Daytonians come from good, solid stock where, when we dream of things to accomplish, we dream big. But we don't just dream. We do. And when we do, we'll see that we can fly as high as we want because we are #daytonstrong.

After all, as Orville Wright once said, "The airplane stays up because it doesn't have time to fail."

And neither do we.

Where Men Learned To Fly

HERBERT WOODWARD MARTIN

In the flat land of Dayton, Ohio
three old gentlemen who controlled
the stones of the streets, the villages,
and their cities, all turned to vast wars
tried looking beneath the winds to
comprehend the prayers and praises
hung there which were invisible to
the naked heart.
We, who were common, who had no
power and came, reverently, to kneel
and hang our own prayers and praises
on the winds like the old men who
had come before us and wrapped
themselves in the salvation of graces
and mysteries hoping to teach us
something to relish about the past.
Now, I am sixty and stand before you,
the future, and all I have as a vision
which is hope and faith. I cannot break
from neither nor bring to it light nor air.
They are the elements with which men
must have if they wish to break free of
the bounds of the earth, to fly, and explore.
The old men realized that the awful grey air
was filled with human infections and that
there was no antidote nor a cure that
would eradicate such desires. No matter
what generosities they offered they had
no solutions, and did not understand
what gravity had done to them.
So, I am content to sing this song of old
prayers and praises to the Gods of
erupting volcanoes to let them know we
understand the knowledge of fire and

realize that it is as necessary as the air.
We seek to know how we can embrace both.
This place will change as we change,
and knowledge will fall upon us as rain
falls on the ground. We are old and shall
not despair for the blood is warn and continues
to flows through our system of changes like
light inhabits the turning earth.
We shall conquer the pull and release of gravity
and free our hearts with tongues and songs.

DAYTON STORIES

The Mad River of Dayton

BETSY HUGHES

The "Hathennithiipi" was the Shawnee name
for this unspoiled, fertile place to fish,
before the frontier's white men ever came
and put down foreign stakes to claim their wish.
When settlers pushing west carved out this town
from wilderness, they chose a watery niche:
A stream from Logan County flowing down
met Great Miami. Such confluence! Rich!
At times its waters flooded, unconfined,
with crazy currents, furious and fast;
its turbulence suggests unfettered mind
which spills past bounds, is visionary, vast.
Creator and destroyer, foe and friend,
Mad River—Lend me passion without end!

The Strange Dual Life of Fannie Tatum

DONNA SWORD

In the winter of 2016, my family was in the maddening position of having to purchase our ancestors' history at an estate sale. After an emotional negotiation with the estate sale agent, I was relieved to have rescued countless vintage photos, letters, and scrapbooks, all of which I spread across my dining room table to review. "What now?" I thought. "Who are these people and what am I going to do with all of them?"

Nothing to do about it but become the self-proclaimed family historian and start doing some research. Do you realize that if you can take your lineage back seven generations, you have 128 fifth-great-grandparents? I didn't. Sure, then start working on your husband's side too, because you have kids who might care someday. It's a research rabbit hole, to be sure, if rabbits named their children the same as all the cousins and maybe bricked up a wall or two along a path. Still, it's so worth it every time a mystery is solved.

Much of our family came to Dayton during the Victorian era, settling here from western Europe. Each of them in turn fell in love, married, and raised their families in the Dayton neighborhoods on Second, Buckeye, Ashley, Warren, and Brown Streets. We discovered an ancestor who made the claim of launching the first daily German-language Dayton newspaper and another was one of the courageous firemen who held the reins of a horse-drawn fire truck to battle the fires during the Great Flood of 1913.

But, in all the research I've done, it was Fannie's story that stood out to me. As one newspaper headline put it, the story of Fannie and Samuel is "worthy of a romance novel." It's a tale of cheating death, then losing the game. A romance trope of star-crossed love found in an unexpected place. And finally, it was a secret fortune followed by a mystery that remains unanswered for over 130 years.

Although separated by three generations, Fannie is a first cousin, as these things go. In the absence of living history and no one left to share her story, we turn to the Victorian era newspapers to tell it for us.

DAYTON, OHIO, November 13. *"As the body lay at the house a carriage drove up and an elegantly dressed lady alighted. Her black eyes, dark hair and features indicated French descent. She hurriedly walked to the front door and excitedly demanded to that she be permitted to see the remains of Mr. Tatum. Her manner was so strange and her agitation so noticeable that this was refused."*

The Chicago Tribune
"An Ohio Romance" November 14, 1887

During the late nineteenth century, Dayton was entering the second industrial revolution, attracting immigrants from Germany, Ireland, Italy, and France who were hoping to escape poverty. The Miami-Erie Canal, which earlier had opened commerce opportunities to other Ohio cities, was becoming outdated as it was replaced by the burgeoning railroad system. And National Cash Register was merely a start-up company, with industrialist John Patterson building his empire on Ritty's invention of the "incorruptible cashier."

Job opportunities were plentiful during this time, especially for any man willing to put in an honest day of labor. It was in this robust economy that Francois Emonnin had arrived from France, met a beautiful Swiss girl named Eugenia, and the two of them planted their roots in Dayton's East Side to work towards the American Dream as it was in Dayton's Victorian era.

Although not wealthy by anyone's measure, the Emonnin family was highly regarded by those who knew them in their working-class neighborhood. Francois, now going as Frank, built his skills to find employment as a journeyman stonecutter. We can imagine him walking the ever-changing downtown streets, pausing to admire the results of his craft in the newly constructed homes and buildings.

So it must have been a startling blow to Frank and Eugenia when they discovered their good name printed in newspapers from Boston to Sioux City when their oldest daughter, Marie Frances, brought scandal to the family.

DAYTON, O., Nov. 13. *"Learning that the lady came from this city an investigation was made here, and a more romantic story than hers would be hard to conceive. She is the daughter of poor but respectable parents."*

The Boston Globe
"Married Her for Love" November 14, 1887

Four years before the Emonnin name became infamous in national news, Marie Frances —called Fannie by her family—was diagnosed with a cancerous tumor. The family spent what little savings they had with doctors in Dayton in attempts to cure their nineteen-year-old daughter, but it wasn't enough. In desperation, Fannie was sent to the Betts Street Hospital in Cincinnati for the Sisters for the Poor of St. Francis to provide her palliative care.

Two remarkable things happened to Fannie while at Betts Street. Whether it was the prayers of the devout Sisters or simply a misdiagnosis of her condition by the nineteenth-century medical community, Fannie fully recovered from her illness. And perhaps just as surprising, she met a young man while hospitalized and fell in love.

Dayton, O., Nov. 14. "*Tatum was but 30 years of age, but was reputed being worth a million at least. He was peculiar in many ways, and by his friends was considered a woman-hater.*"

Evening Star, Washington, DC
"*A Millionaire's Secret Marriage*" November 15, 1887

Samuel C. Tatum, Jr., the son of a prominent Cincinnati businessman, was the favored heir to his father's fortune. Samuel's reputation among the polite society of Cincinnati was that of a confirmed bachelor, a situation that was surely frustrating to the young ladies of the Queen City's elite who had their eye on one of the most eligible bachelors around.

So, we wonder, what was it about Fannie that finally turned the head of the contrary Mr. Tatum? Was it how her dark eyes reflected the candle's light as they talked on into the evenings? Or maybe that sing-song accent that held a hint of her western European heritage? Perhaps all it took was the attention of a poor French girl from Dayton who was so very different from the women of society he knew so well and despised even more.

Within six months they were married, but under the fictitious names of Herbert Linton and Fannie Thresher. Samuel was insistent to keep his marriage a secret from his parents; they weren't to know about his union with this working-class daughter of immigrants. They rented an apartment on Court Street in Cincinnati and kept house as Mr. and Mrs. Linton. Cincinnati's City Directory listed Samuel's occupation as bookkeeper, but this was just another falsehood to give credence to his second life. Samuel continued to work as a superintendent at his father's business at the Sam'l C. Tatum Co., a prosperous iron foundry and machine works on Reading

Road. Samuel would alternatively live in both homes, telling the other family he was traveling for business.

> Dayton special to New York *World*. *"It appears that Fannie had her doubts about that sort of marriage and pleaded with her liege lord that they get married by their proper names. This he promised, but refused to have it take place in Cincinnati."*
> The Inter Ocean, Chicago IL
> *"A Millionaire's Dual Life"* November 19, 1887

After a time, Fannie found this duplicitous life hard to bear. Their only child died as an infant, bringing Fannie to feel a profound isolation from her family. She was ready to reveal the marriage and yet couldn't break Samuel's trust by allowing his parents to discover his second life. They came to a compromise of sorts. Samuel agreed to meet Fannie's family, but only as Herbert Linton. This wasn't enough for Fannie. They made a trip to the east, stopping in Buffalo, New York, where they registered for a new marriage certificate. And on July 5, 1885, Marie Frances Emonnin was legally wed to Samuel C. Tatum, Jr. She had no way to know at the time how this one decision would change the course of her life.

As with the first marriage certificate, Samuel agreed to the formality only to placate Fannie's anxieties. The two continued their quiet lives as the Lintons in their Cincinnati home. Samuel made true on his promise to meet Fannie's parents and they visited often to the Emonnin's tidy shotgun-style home on East Second Street, just a block away from the Miami-Erie canal and Dayton & Michigan railroad tracks. During these visits, Fannie would sometimes slip and call her husband Samuel, not Herbert, but at this her mother merely shrugged it off as one of her daughter's many quirks.

Then four years after Fannie's implausible recovery at Betts Street Hospital, Samuel fell seriously ill. The doctors came and went and did what they could. But as always with Fannie's life story, it wasn't enough.

On November 8, 1887, Samuel C. Tatum, Jr., the heir to a fortune, died of the common man's affliction of typhoid fever. Fannie was twenty-four years old and a widow. She had no choice now but to reveal their dual lives; this heavy secret they kept together for the last four years. All of it and to everyone.

> DAYTON, OHIO, November 14. *"A particularly interesting affair has come to light since the recent death of Samuel C. Tatum, a young*

millionaire of Avondale, an aristocratic suburb of Cincinnati."
Wilkes-Barre Times Leader
"A Strange Dual Life" November 14, 1887

The story is told that Fannie was unaware of her husband's wealth. It's said that she discovered this secret on the morning she appeared on the doorstep of his parents' manor with the New York marriage certificate tucked in the pocket of her black mourning dress. Whether this is truth or lore, it was indeed a fact that Fannie was an heir to Samuel's wealth, due to her insistence for a marriage document in their legal names. The French girl who was from a poor, but respectable family, lost her true love to inherit $25,000 in personalty – about $675,000 by today's numbers. The young Samuel neglected to write a will, so Fannie didn't inherit any real estate property. However, she did have the right of "realty for life," which allowed her to live in the Tatum family's manor along with Samuel's mother and sisters. Fannie declined.

A card from Mr. Tatum's Brother-in-Law. *"To the Editor of the* Enquirer. *Your account of to-day's paper of the marriage and funeral of Samuel C. Tatum, jun., is of so sensational a character, and contains some statements so at variance with the truth, that we insist, in justice to all concerned, that the following statement of facts shall be given as much prominence as that to to-day's narration … I regret that you should thus have added to the sorrows of the widow and the family of the dead by such unfortunate statements."*
The Cincinnati Enquirer
"Like a Romance" November 14, 1887

Many prominent newspapers during the Victorian era employed a narrative style to share the day's news with their readers. Beyond the who, what, where, and how that we're accustomed to reading today, some editors at that time preferred a more colorful verse to inform citizens of the goings on within their fair city. This may have encouraged some correspondents to embellish just a bit to build a dramatic effect. Samuel Hilles, the husband of Samuel's sister, Amy, took issue with this liberty of the facts in a public way by way of letter to the editor of the *Cincinnati Enquirer.*

It was true, Samuel Hilles admitted, that the Tatum family was unaware of the marriage—at least until Samuel Tatum was on his deathbed. As readers of Mr. Hilles' letter, we can be comforted to know that Samuel

C. Tatum, Jr. was among his family—his mother, sister, and beloved young wife—when he released his last breath. And this happened upon the marriage bed in the home he made with Fannie.

The rest of Fannie's story is unfortunately lost to history as many of these tales are. After Samuel's death, Fannie returned to Dayton to live with one of her brothers and his wife, but any public record of her after 1890 has not been found. So, in the absence of facts, we are provided the luxury to imagine on her behalf.

Of course, being a young woman, she could have very likely married again and carried on her life into the twentieth century with a lovely house and many dark-eyed children that looked just like her. Or instead, we might choose to see her taking her small fortune to venture out in style to the wild and untamed west for new adventures befitting her uncommon spirit.

Or the saddest ending of all to imagine, it is possible that Fannie may have been admitted at Dayton's State Hospital (the former Dayton Asylum for the Insane), as her father, Frank, was in 1894 when he was declared a victim of lunacy by Dayton's probate court. In a time when even a sustained state of melancholy would be a cause for commitment, wealth wouldn't be enough to save a young woman. Which, of course, would complete the theme of Fannie's life of *not enough*.

We'll keep hoping for that happy ending though, won't we? After all, Fannie deserves as much from those of us who know her story.

Ode to the Banks of a River in Dayton, Ohio 1913

MATTHEW L. SZOZDA

Is this still a city that sells blood down the river?
A landscape built by blue-collar sing-alongs
Stolen from flight and factories and poems?

When floodwaters buried the doors of the 5th Street Deli,
Were we reborn on the banks of segregation and opioids?
How does one begin to classify a natural disaster?
Is this not also the gentrification of our neighborhoods?

Can a river be anything other than a wall of privilege? Perhaps an ocean
in midnight light?
Perhaps she does not have to show up alone
But instead she carries the bodies of her people
Onto the edge of a tide until we all are floating bottle ships.

Until salt holds our hardened skin in its hands
And softens us back into children.
Until we all have mothers and fathers again.
Until Ohio glows through the concrete in our eyes
And the current no longer runs red.

So on the nights when this city decides to love me
Or fucks me.
She will know
I am not yet finished.

A Strong Man in Dayton's History: Lee Warren James

MERLE WILBERDING

The term "Dayton Strong" accurately describes our Dayton community in 2019, as together we have endured tornadoes that wiped out major sections of Dayton's residential and business districts; we have endured a Ku Klux Klan rally that disrupted our community and cost the City of Dayton almost $1,000,000 to manage and withstand; and we have endured a mass shooting in the Oregon District that left nine people dead and another twenty-seven people injured. These are tough times that will leave lasting pain and fear, but we remain grateful how well the Dayton community has pulled together with the endearing "Dayton Strong" mantra.

But this is a mantra that Dayton has earned over its more than 200-year history. And each time Dayton needed to be strong, there were men and women who rose to the occasion. Certainly, there have been many strong voices and strong leaders in 2019, just as there were in other times of community trauma, like the Dayton flood of 1913, when John Patterson, the owner of the National Cash Register, personally led the recovery efforts after the flood.

Readers may recall that the Dayton flood inundated the city from March 21 through March 26, 1913, as a winter rainstorm dumped 8 to 11 inches of rain onto the saturated ground. The ensuing runoff engulfed the city, causing 360 deaths and multi-millions of dollars in destruction.

To compound the flood calamity, the City of Dayton had been experiencing severe deficits for years, in part because it continued to issue more and more municipal bonds to cover its operating and personal expenditures. To combat this growing problem, a 100-person Citizens Committee had been set up in 1912 to consider alternatives that might then become possible under the new "Home Rule" authority created by an amendment to the State of Ohio Constitution.

Under the proposed city manager form of government, the city council would be responsible for enacting legislation for appropriations and public improvements, but the administration of the city would be controlled by a city manager who would serve at the pleasure of the city commission.

As it turned out the vote on the adoption of the proposed city manager form of government came shortly after the flood and it was approved in part because many people believed that the city's government had failed in its response to the flood. The result was that the city manager form of government was adopted by a 2:1 majority on August 12, 1913. As an historical point, Dayton was the first large city in the United States to adopt the city manager form of government, and to many Dayton had become the model for its adoption by many other cities throughout the United States.

That 100-person Citizens Committee was chaired by Lee Warren James, a local lawyer who played a key part in the adoption of the city manager form of government. At the time James was the law director of the City of Dayton which was then a part-time position. James chaired the Citizens Committee and was significantly involved in the drafting of the city manager charter.

Looking back at Lee Warren James and his contribution to the strength of Dayton's city manager form of government, his accomplishments are even more extraordinary. While he is identified as the law director of the City of Dayton, that was really a part-time job, as he continued his private practice. Although identified as a practicing lawyer, that does not tell the whole story. Lee Warren James never went to college. He never went to law school. No. After graduating from Steele High School, he immediately started studying law in the office of Oscar Gottschall.

Teeming with the self-confidence that seemed to propel his entire career, in 1900 Lee Warren James moved from his apprentice position with Oscar Gottschall to the then pre-eminent law firm of Rowe & Shuey. Soon thereafter, he sat for and passed the Ohio bar exam. By 1916 the Rowe & Shuey firm morphed into James & Coolidge, a name that would continue for the next twenty years. (Even now, the name "Coolidge" remains an integral part of the Coolidge Wall firm as it continues its law practice.)

Lee Warren James was a powerful and commanding figure, with broad shoulders, a thick-set chest, and a Hollywood aura about him—perhaps a James Cagney aura. In fairness to James, the Olympian stature reflected Olympian talent. He was known as a brilliant business lawyer, but he was equally adept in the courtroom.

On the business side, he was a member of the board of directors of Winters National Bank (which would first merge into Bank One, N.A., and later become part of JPMorgan Chase). When the National Cash Register Co. went public in 1926, Lee Warren James played an integral role in working with Frederick Patterson (the son of John Patterson) and three company managers who made a substantial profit from the public offering. Indeed, Lee Warren James reportedly netted over $1,000,000 in 1926 dollars from the transaction.

On the courtroom side, he had extraordinary success, including arguing many cases in front of the Ohio Supreme Court—many of them about the limits of the "home rule" authority. He even argued one case in front of the United States Supreme Court, *Dale v. Pattison*, a case which determined the bankruptcy lien rights to more than one hundred barrels of Mudlick Whiskey, a popular bourbon that had been produced by the David Rohrer Distillery in Germantown.

Beginning with his education at Steele High School and continuing throughout his career, Lee Warren James used his talents and skills to play a vital role in the establishment of the city manager form of government for the City of Dayton. He played an integral part of National Cash Register becoming a public company and being able to expand its operations throughout the world. And, he had the legal acumen and rhetoric to argue a significant case before the United States Supreme Court. Lee Warren James was truly a strong man in Dayton's history

Higher

MARY COMBS

The garage door boomed like a kettle drum.
Windows shivered in their frames.
Somewhere overhead a needle-nosed jet
Shattered the sound barrier into fragments of air,
That bounced off our homes and
Rattled our ribs.

Arms outstretched,
We took off from our swings and
The top of the slide,
Flying our own skinny bodies
Around the backyard
On red sneakers and root beer Kool Aid.

At the end of sleepy drives back home
We watched for the chain of blue lights
Marking the flight line along Airway Road.
A mile away our grandfather
Had hopped off the interurban
At Simms Station
To see Wilbur test the Wright Flyer with
Careful loops around the honey locust tree
In the middle of Huffman Field.

White contrails criss-crossed
The bright blue sky above us in
Shining kisses,
Only a decade after
That shy bachelor Orville's heart gave out.
A decade later men would watch earthrise
From the Sea of Tranquility.

Now we listen for purposeful spikes
In the hum of cosmic radiation.

Our children watch planets lit by earth's sun
Journey across the starfield,
And they dream.

The Houses Which Populate Dayton

HERBERT WOODWARD MARTIN

The plaster in these houses will peel
long before the land or the citizens
begin to peel, and they will do it slowly
for they have not learned the swiftness
of death pealing but the flesh knows it.
you can see the shale fall from the houses;
the pieces, colorfully, falling away as the
foundations merge with the skins. And
another color and foundation are merged
together. What children will turn into
inheritors and reach out to breath in the
land? The exteriors of these domiciles
are the results of a war of changes; the
interiors remain a cracked porcelain, and
the collector of ancestral dust.

Arcade

BILL VERNON

I was anxious because John Torvich had promised to introduce me to a girl. I pushed through two heavy swinging doors on Ludlow Street and faced the glare of wild, dead eyes. Fish of every description were lined up in ice trays: catfish, walleye, perch, and others I couldn't name, more fish than I'd ever seen together, many of them exotic for Dayton. Cod, trout, white fish, salmon, and crabs, all "FRESH" the signs claimed. "Flown in today." Noticing their colors and shapes, I hurried on, imagining how they'd look in their native waters, swimming around.

Where was he? I circled inside the Arcade's street-level circle, checking the small groups of shoppers around the four-wheeled vendors selling popcorn, caramel-covered nuts, soft drinks, and hotdogs. No Torvich. I looked above as if he might be there. Through the glass dome, sunlight streamed in to spotlight some of the brightly painted decorations below each railing on the third and second floors, large acorns, apples, bunches of grapes, sheep, wild turkeys, and sheaves of wheat. No Torvich up there.

My watch showed I was ten minutes late. He'd probably given up on me.

I hurried into McCrory's. Sure enough there was Torvich seated at the counter among a crowd of Julienne girls (blue uniforms), St. Joseph's girls (green uniforms), and two of my classmates (white shirts and ties). He waved at me from his seat, pointed at his watch, then returned to talking to someone.

I sat on a stool at the edge of the group and ordered a cherry Coke with French fries and ketchup. The two nearest girls smiled and said hi, but other than that we didn't speak. Except for the boys, they were all strangers to me. Torvich had said he'd introduce me to a brunette, someone I'd like, but there were several brunettes here so which one he'd meant I didn't know.

Some of the boys and girls spun on their mushroom-shaped seats and sang along with pop songs that played on the small silver juke boxes before them. The sounds their coins bought were tinny and thin, but the music was clear enough to create a mood. Some of the boys sucked on Lucky Strikes and Camels. With some fanfare, one of the bolder girls lit up too.

A waitress counted change to a man two seats away, a man and a woman standing behind me discussed problems in their office, NCR cash registers rang as drawers opened and slammed. Laborers in work clothes, white collar workers in suits, and dressed-up matrons fingered clothing hung on racks or five-and-dime-store doodads displayed on metal shelves.

My problem was that the kids at the counter had all gone through elementary schools together. They were friends from way back. I was from out of town, Lebanon, twenty-five miles down Cincinnati Pike (Route 48) and didn't know places, events, or people they talked about.

I kept checking my watch. At thirty minutes until my bus left, someone wasted a nickel on the oldie, "Ain't That A Shame." I wallowed in its two-minute celebration of sadness, but that resulted in the song's repeating in my mind like a throbbing headache while I hustled along the crowded sidewalks to catch my Greyhound at the bus station on First Street.

Originally published as "Out Of Place" in Zest Lit, *February 2015.*

We Ran Into The Future Like We Knew The Way

TERRY FOCHT

It was the early 60s in Dayton, Ohio.
Teenagers and college kids alike
were looking to define themselves.

We were searching for our voice.
We were searching to find our way.

We were not sure what we were doing,
but we knew we were destined to do it.

History tells us that every sixty years or so there is a revolution.
It looked like our youth was claiming its turn.

Dayton's youth marched, protested, sat down and sat in.
We Ran Into The Future Like We Knew The Way.

Our souls leaped, our souls cried.
We cried for the joy of the day.
We cried for the misery of the day.
We were searching for who we were,
and who we could be.

The days passed slowly… the times flew by.
We questioned everything.
Could we rise to the top by diving deeper?

It was the start, we thought, of a freer time,
a better time, a more loving time,
yet, a more rebellious time.

The establishment was at 6.4 on the Richter scale,
shaking in fear of what was coming.

The 60s were exploding.

There were thousands of causes and movements.
Many worthwhile, many not.
Many now forgotten,
some not forgiven.

Inclusion was gaining its place,
for many too fast,
for many too slow.

Oh God, for many too slow.

War loomed like a tornado in the background,
like a hurricane in our conscience.

There was a division in our city,
Our country,
confusion in our brains,
a volcanic eruption to our peace.

Boys became men by going to war.
Boys became men by not.

Many friends went to battle.
Many came back.
Too many did not.

Many never to be whole again.

We lost a president.
The nation cried.
The world cried.

Everyone got older that day.
It was harder to breath.

We were a nation divided…
A nation at war…

At war with our enemies,
our elders,
ourselves,
the establishment,

We were at war with war.

We prayed for Peace,
for the innocence of our youth.

We Ran Into The Future Like We Knew The Way.

The Heart of College Basketball

PETER TITLEBAUM AND JOSEPH GARDNER

My name is Peter Titlebaum, or as my students call me, Doc T. I have been a college professor, teaching sports management, for more than twenty-five years. In my office is a framed set of basketball cards of my favorite team, the New York Knicks, from their 1969-70 NBA championship season.

What does this have to do with Dayton, Ohio? On that celebrated team was a Dayton Flyer—Donnie May, a two-time consensus All-American. I grew up in Rochester, New York, so with the Knicks as my cause célèbre, I had a small connection to the University of Dayton even back then. Today, I take great pride in educating and explaining the connection between Dayton and the National Collegiate Athletic Association (NCAA), and how the city of Dayton wove itself into the fabric of college basketball.

Dayton has long had a rich basketball tradition. In 1947, UD hired Tom Blackburn as its head coach. He held the reins until 1964, establishing the Flyers as a college basketball force while his team compiled a 352-141 record. Don Donoher took over after Blackburn passed away and held the head coaching post for twenty-five years. He helped maintain the Flyers' prominence, delivering a 437-275 record.

Everyone at the University knew that consistent winning records would help increase the value of the UD brand. However, winning basketball games was never going to be enough in the mind of one Dayton visionary.

Imagine telling your boss that, because stands were full at the Fieldhouse (which housed basketball games prior to 1969) with a capacity of 5,500, they would need to build an arena that would hold 2 1/2 times that crowd. Not only would an arena of this size establish the University as a great place for basketball, it would position UD favorably for years to come since the NCAA needed venues to hold its annual college basketball tournament. Athletic director Thomas Frericks was the man with this vision, one he formulated in 1967 to lay the foundation for a mid-sized city in Southwest Ohio to have a lasting impact on college basketball at a national scale.

The Dayton area was already recently familiar with college basketball success when Frericks proposed his idea to build an arena just off the University's campus. Prior to 1967, the Flyers had won the National Invitation Tournament once (1962) and finished as runner-up five times. Frericks saw the opportunities that college basketball was providing to other cities hosting tournaments and he wanted Dayton to be included.

Two years after the Flyers' 1967 runner-up NCAA tournament run, the $4.5 million project reached completion and the UD Arena began to host tournament games. In its first season playing in UD Arena, 1969–70, the Flyers men's basketball team averaged 12,982 fans per game, not far off the new stadium's capacity. This record stood for forty-seven seasons. In the 2016–17 Flyers attendance topped the 13,000 mark, averaging 13,018 fans (97%) per game. The "Flyer Faithful," as UD's fans are known, have consistently shown their support and pride since the arena's opening, placing UD in the NCAA Division I Top 25 in men's basketball attendance for most of the last fifty years.

The near-overnight success of UD basketball and the UD Arena led to the NCAA awarding Dayton the 1970 Mideast Regional quarterfinal games. But this was no surprise to Frericks. Always proactive in his role as UD athletic director, Frericks was a major catalyst in bringing the tournament to Dayton. To ensure its return, he continued to seek opportunities to work with the NCAA in more meaningful ways. He began serving on the Division I men's basketball committee in 1987 and became chair in 1992. Unfortunately, Frericks would only spend one season as chair before passing away in January 1992 from cancer.

His was a great foundation upon which to build, but it was not going to be easy. Times were changing, and if Dayton was not careful it could find itself on the outside looking in, as many schools and communities were building bigger venues. But the NCAA Tournament's expansion also played a critical role in Dayton's rise. From 1969 to 1985, the men's basketball tournament expanded from twenty-two to sixty-four teams, delivering more hosting opportunities to UD Arena.

Ted Kissell continued UD's relationship with the NCAA when he took over as director of athletics, holding the position for sixteen years before stepping down at the end of 2008. During his tenure, Kissell followed Frericks' blueprint, overseeing twenty-six tournament games.

The real game changer came in 2001 when the tournament expanded to sixty-five teams and added an opening-round game unofficially known as the "play-in game," which Dayton was selected to host. Why Dayton? UD was already hosting six games that year, so adding one more was simple enough. The venue was also close to NCAA headquarters in Indianapolis, and UD had proven its worth over the years with its relationship with the NCAA.

Selection Sunday is the name of the event in which the NCAA reveals the bracket for that year's tournament. The play-in game took place on Tuesday, two days after Selection Sunday, and matched up the two lowest-ranking teams in the field. The winner then advanced to play the number one seed in that region.

The NCAA wanted the student-athletes in the play-in game to have an NCAA experience. Unfortunately, if you find out on Sunday that your team will be playing in Dayton on Tuesday, it's unlikely many of your fans are able to attend the game.

This is where Dayton stepped up. Even if these schools could not bring many of their own fans to the game, Dayton was determined to make it a great experience for the visiting athletes. Most of these basketball teams had never played in front of so many fans or at an arena this large—but in Dayton, the joke is if you simply toss a basketball into UD Arena, 10,000 people are going to show up and watch.

And they did.

Kissell also oversaw numerous capital investments and structural improvements to the arena, which helped demonstrate to the NCAA both the university and city commitment to college basketball, as well as the importance of hosting the tournament.

In 2009, Tim Wabler took over as athletic director at UD and continued his predecessors' work. He oversaw thirty-four men's tournament games from 2009–15, including the inception of the First Four in 2011. Due to its successful decade of hosting the play-in game coupled with the other factors mentioned, Dayton won the bid to host the First Four, which expanded the tournament to sixty-eight teams and sent eight teams to play four games in Dayton on Tuesday and Wednesday, before the first round began at other sites on Thursday.

The University used this opportunity to form a partnership with the First Four Local Organizing Committee, a coalition of local businesses and civic organizations, creating even greater community involvement with NCAA events than ever before. After a successful four-year run, UD was awarded the First Four from 2015–18 and again won hosting rights through 2022.

Arena renovations have played a large role in helping secure these contracts. In May 2017, UD's current athletic director, Neil Sullivan, and president, Eric F. Spina, announced a $72 million renovation that was completed in 2019, the fourth in UD Arena's history. The first took place in 1998, when the Donoher Center (named after UD's storied head coach) was added. The Donoher Center is attached to the main arena and houses the men's and women's locker rooms as well as administration offices. The second renovation came in 2002, when luxury suites, lounges, and video boards were added at a cost of $13.1 million. The property underwent its third renovation in 2015, when locker rooms, training rooms, offices and other amenities were updated at a cost of $4 million.

Nothing in sports is ever guaranteed. Dayton is trying to stay relevant in the eyes of the NCAA, always focusing on the future while ensuring its multi-use arena meets the highest standards in event hosting. UD Arena celebrated its fiftieth anniversary in 2019, and while the University has won a guarantee to host the First Four through 2022, that doesn't mean it will continue to have that opportunity indefinitely. The need to evolve and change is critical as venues across the country continue to improve.

It is this writer's belief if all things are equal, the NCAA will do everything in its power to keep the First Four in Dayton. However, if Dayton ever assumes it to be their event and no longer seeks to meet the NCAA's level of expectations, it will be lost. Sports is about making money and the chosen venue must remain competitive in today's age.

Having seen the Flyer Faithful in action during my time at UD, I am confident that this won't happen. The pride this community takes in hosting this event shows how badly they want it. Nobody is going to take it away.

At the end of 2019, UD Arena had hosted the most NCAA Tournament games ever with 125. No one else comes close.

The Downtown Dayton Depot

BILL VERNON

In the long-gone Greyhound bus station on First Street, announcements boomed as if God were speaking from a big black box attached among painted-on wispy white clouds to the high blue ceiling. "The bus for Los Angeles is now loading at Gate Four. Passengers from New York please re-board at this time." These names echoed loudly, along with others like Toronto, Detroit, Dallas, and Atlanta, suggesting that I choose them as a destination instead of home. Going and coming, starting and ending were in the air. Like a gale, the desire to run away to other cities pumped adrenaline through me although I had no real choice. The mysterious nature of each distant place was a lure that would often distract me.

The building was cathedral-like, ovate and spacious, with corners and other sharp edges rounded off. It dwarfed me, waiting for my summons. Limbo-like, it gathered people temporarily, promising to deliver them eventually to a better place. The angel on duty was a toothless old man with two piles of his stock-in-trade on the floor beside him, the *Dayton Journal Herald* morning newspaper and the *Dayton Daily News* afternoon. Both versions of the world were five cents a copy six days a week. The *Journal* took a day off on the Christian Sabbath. This wingless patriarch always centered himself among the four long, back-to-back rows of shiny wooden pews, and through their aisles pilgrims rushed past forlornly, elatedly, angrily, indifferently, mood apparent in their expressions and movements.

I sat facing the exit to the buses as if afraid mine might escape without me unless I watched. The old man's preferred throne faced the street doors and therefore me. As a lonely freshman exiled from a high school ten blocks away, I watched his grubby hands take donations and dispense nickels, dimes and quarters. Gradually he began to recognize me. We said only hi for weeks. Then one day he said, "You got marble eyes. They look right through me."

Feeling like an altar boy who'd somehow failed to serve correctly during mass, I said, "Oh? I'm sorry." Maybe I was rudely staring at him more than I realized.

His comment had exploded into the open as if his tolerance had reached its limit. A victim of social dysfunction myself, and so interested in the condition, I imagined nervous resentment building up inside the man's mind until reaching a critical mass it had to be released suddenly and decisively. It was the clearest thing I ever heard him say.

His habitual glances up at whoever walked past limited our occasional conversations. He'd stop talking as he looked away, or I'd see that he was ignoring me and swallow my words. Both circumstances required repetitions of what had been said before. Even worse, a speech impediment limited the old man's clarity. His words oozed together so his sentences rumbled from his mouth with each phoneme imperfectly formed. He needed teeth to structure his sunken cheeks and shape his tongue. Then he might have sculpted sounds into recognizable pronunciations.

Catching just a word here and there, I guessed at what he tried to convey: that his son had abandoned him and Ohio, moving to Kentucky, leaving the old man alone in a nearby room alongside the wide but shallow Great Miami River. His wife had died on him. His occupation as a house painter ended when he fell off a ladder and injured his back. That's what I thought I knew of his life. He was hard of hearing so asking for verification of my understanding would have required complicated, very loud questions among a crowd of strangers. I was too timid to pursue the truth. So he'd mumble, I'd nod, make a noise, and our talks were brief.

Sitting there on a bench, reading Chaminade's high school textbooks, scribbling short essay assignments, translating Virgil, or reviewing notes, I'd sometimes look up, notice a benevolent glint in his eyes, and think of statues of Christ and his cohorts watching me and my classmates with similar approval during our required visits to church. Like those depictions of holy men and women, the old guy seemed to be forgiving me for my silence and culpability. My response to him was unconscious, unexpressed, but perhaps predictable, something nuns had choreographed for me to do since first communion: an urge to kneel before him and confess.

Originally appeared as "Depot," Sprout Magazine, July 15, 2014

The Northtown Bar and Grill

JOHN GORMAN

We ate at the Northtown Bar & Grill almost every Saturday of my childhood,
As often as possible, as far back as I can remember. After CYO basketball or
Ahead of an empty teenage afternoon, I'd play darts or pinball while
Mom and Dad held court with family and friends stopping by for
A sandwich and a conversation. They made great chili and better burgers,
Everything on the menu tasted the way that it should, and we always had
The same waitress, an older lady named Annie who worked there
Or in places like it—joints with vinyl booths and wood paneling and
Thin carpeting in which you didn't want to find yourself too long after
The sun went down—longer than our parents had known each other.
The building was a house, really, with the bar on one end in
What would've been the front parlor and the kitchen in back of
A dining area that would've been the living room. We'd meet there
Most Saturdays, from around 11 AM until around 1 PM, and
Annie would take our orders and bring the food, us kids would
Eat sandwiches and play bar games, and our parents would
Have lunch and a few drinks while taking stock and enjoying the company.
At the end of it, Dad liked to pay with a personal check,
From which Annie happily made change.

One Wednesday when I was nineteen, I stopped in by myself on a
Lonely lunch hour taken from my summer job mowing lawns and
Clearing brush for my old man. Some days friends worked with me
But not that one, and when I got hungry I figured, it's right over there,
And I would love a cup of chili, not to mention that burger, and
A round or two of darts, why not? The place was empty,
Save four or five forlorn men along the rail in the front parlor bar
Not saying much of anything to one another while drinking draft beer
From those old glasses pinched near the bottom and billowed out
To the rim. I waved to Annie behind the bar on my way in and
She glared at me as I took a seat in the deserted dining area so familiar from
Those Saturdays, except the details that day didn't match up,
The overhead lights off and the dartboard and pinball machine unplugged,
Though the video poker cubby was going, a crushed cigarette burning itself out

In a red ash tray beside it. Annie hurried to where I sat and asked,
"What are you doing here?" I smiled and said, "I was hoping for a cheeseburger."
She shook her head, blinked twice, and said, "Kitchen's closed, son,"
And then, "Get on out of here, and don't come back without your daddy."

The Northtown was on Main Street, about halfway between our home
On the north side and downtown, at the heart of a commercial district that,
When I was a kid, had lots of stores and businesses, and through which
Life and commerce chugged for years and nobody noticed a thing,
Not with so much going on, not with so much work to do. But when I left
That Wednesday, I looked around, and I did notice. Lots of things.
The following Saturday we met Dad there and the Northtown was full,
The sun was out, the area aglow with that gilded Dayton loveliness,
In spite of all the drooping wires, in spite of the cracked and gashed pavement,
In spite of the almost entirely abandoned nearby shopping center, which
Partnered well with the strip mall across Main and down a ways
In not-much-better condition. Lunch went the way it always did, Annie
Taking our orders and bringing the food and the rest of us doing our things.
She didn't say a word about my visit that Wednesday, either, but there was
A look she gave me once, short and pointed, over top of my mother's head.

The Northtown isn't there anymore. Don't bother looking for it.
Someone bought the property, razed the building, paved the lot.
Nothing took its place, and the surrounding area never quite recovered
From the beating it took at the end of the twentieth century. Most of the
Corpses have been cleared from the battlefield, at least, and they
Re-paved Main there, too. The stage is set for whatever comes next,
But now when we're all in town we don't know what to do on Saturdays.
We'll sit around and talk as everyone stares at their phones and tablets,
Sometimes make sandwiches, sometimes have a drink. A few people
Come by to visit, but there aren't as many folks around as there used to be.
Some are dead, some are sick, some moved away, some lost touch.
We'll watch TV, but it's so big, and so loud, it can be hard to handle.
There's a basketball hoop out back, but no dart boards or pinball, and
There are a dozen fast food joints by the highway exit that are supposed to
Count for something. We can't figure out what that is.

The Spouse Test

JESSE MULLEN

We sit alone on the second-floor balcony of a dilapidated studio on Greenwood, just south of South Park. Breathe in the hot humid air. Ignore our three dirty camp-wear dishes stacked next to the sink, our Meijer air mattress with a slow leak that works as an unofficial alarm waking us when our shoulder and hip shout to turn over from the pressure of hardwood floors and body weight. There's a laundry in the basement, but dirty sheets can wait.

We still have a clean shirt, socks, boxer-briefs. There's a yellow and blue can of foot spray near the shoes on the stairs. Soon we'll take a cold shower, wash away the sticky sweat of last night's drinking, flip through the pictures on our phone, listen to old voicemails and get dressed.

But for now we'll lean against the cracked, rotting railing of the balcony. We'll stare into the woods at our left, at a fallen tree on a crushed mud porch on our right, and down to the yard, covered in tiny dirt mounds upon which dozens of bright yellow and black monsters peacefully crawl waiting for their noisy dessert.

Menthols make the pounding subside. Pain abates, but pressure remains, not overly physical but from an unsettled knowledge that tomorrow will be the same and then not.

Not unfamiliar, still unpleasant.

We dread the chirps of an incoming email, call, or text, at least most of the time. Occasionally, the calls are magic, a laugh, giggle, cry, whine, boredom, happiness, anger, from a tiny girl three states away wondering where we are. But mostly the calls are anger.

Anger and urgency.

For now it's still.

Let's stand and stretch, turn and walk to the door that sticks. Inside it's stale, but clean enough. Our phone goes in a pocket, wallet in another and a cool blast of refrigeration hits as we scan the mayo, sauces and salad mix slowly rotting in a drawer.

Today we'll drive up the hill and find a home for the family that's not there. It's squat with bricks, a cracked driveway, trees and grass and chain-link fence. The neighbor's nice at least at first. In this house our family will grow, in size and apart. A boy will join the tiny girl, not fixing what we thought. They'll leave, then stay, we'll sneak away to drink and to work. The work will go well, the home life less so, so we'll try another fix, further south to Springboro.

·

Wild Irish Rose (Dayton, Ohio 2001)

DREW PERFILIO

the Wayne Ave. bus stop brims with
parentheticals: drunkards perverts
holy motherfuckers icons and cigarette butts
it's cooler here in the shadows of emptied warehouses
-falling brick and mortar shells-
terrific reminders that
we are only what we contain within us.
the body (after all) is just a container for the soul
and it seems to me this part of the city is
soul-sick sleeping and only half alive

down the block on third st.
they sell lotto tickets coffee
and bottles of Wild Irish Rose
to people who are only trying to purchase hope.
outside Wympee's diner an old drunk
has to borrow my nickel to scratch his five-dollar ticket.
"hey man you wanna swig off my brick'a Rose?"
he says in place of "thank you"
and as he down the rest of the bottle
he praises Jesus for his luck
he praises Jesus for the good years in Webster Station.
all he wins is another ticket
he keeps the nickel
he stares across the blvd. that once was a canal
he stare across the city blocks stretched out
i can only guess what he see across the acres of tarmac:
maybe an old Studebaker
maybe one of the dozens of theaters
that once dotted this city
maybe he sees the ghosts of commerce and industry
    a Delco factory

the Gentile Produce Company
Lorenz Music Publishing
McCrory's Five and Dime
maybe he sees that city of neighborhoods
before they cut her heart with an interstate
and let it bleed into pools of suburbs.

but all i can see
are his eyes
full and bright and burdened with tears
recalling the dumpsters behind Race St.
full of broken bottles broken memories broken desires.
the causes of so many mornings after
and just a few inspired words
spoken softly as his tears spill onto his cheeks
"can ya spare some more change
fer jus' one more brick'a Rose?"
and i give in 'cause
i'm a coward a guilty fool and scared as hell
that one day i'll wake up to find
i don't recognize anything around me

as he walks back into the diner his tears dry up
he smiles he praises Jesus once again
but he never thanks me.
i walk away into the city that has forgotten him
toward the tourist attractions
and the newly minted ballpark
out of one man's history and into another's.
sometimes life just like "progress"
is climbing a ladder laid sideways
trying to build a new city
on a cracked foundation
an imagined future on the broken back of the past
is just one more brick'a Rose
for an incurable drunk

Who Killed John Crawford?

ERIC RHODES

I was mulling over my senior thesis topic at Antioch College in the summer of 2014 when John Crawford was killed. Crawford, an unarmed black man, was shot down at the Beavercreek Walmart by a cop. A white woman called the police and complained that he was carrying a BB gun up and down the aisles. Crawford had picked the gun up at the store and it was still in its packaging. I wanted to know how Beavercreek, like so many suburbs, had created this deadly and violent fear in the woman. I wanted to know how Beavercreek became so white, so relatively affluent, and so afraid. And I wanted to know more about segregation and how its effects extended to black people living throughout the Miami Valley.

I consulted the statistics. The Dayton metropolitan area was the fifteenth most segregated in the nation in 2010—with the majority of the black population living in West Dayton. I learned that this segregation also had a deleterious economic effect where black people lived in the Miami Valley. By 2010, Dayton had the fourth highest concentration of poverty among African Americans of any major U.S. city, and West Dayton was one of America's largest food deserts. How did this come to pass? I decided to go to the archives to find out.

The noted scholar of African American studies Dr. Manning Marable, recounting his childhood during the 1950s, wrote that Dayton consisted of "two parallel racial universes which cohabited the same city." Dr. Marable's recollection that "African Americans generally resided west of the Great Miami River" applies about as equally today as it did then.

Racial discrimination, not natural proclivity, made the west side black and the east side white. Beginning in the 1910s, black migrants trickled into Dayton, seeking refuge from racial violence and economic misery in the South. But they found that Dayton's movie theaters and public transportation were segregated too. That same decade, the federal government began bolstering lending practices which forbade banks from granting mortgages to black families outside of West Dayton. Lending institutions and the government redlined and impoverished black neighborhoods. At the same time, they kept white neighborhoods white and middle class by enforcing racially restrictive covenants throughout the interwar years.

Dayton's shift to a wartime economy in the 1940s drew even larger numbers of black Southerners to the city. After the Second World War, the Veterans Administration underwrote white flight to new suburban homes while West Dayton remained overcrowded with an aging housing stock. Poor Appalachian families on the east side were given keys to one-car garages, but their fellow black migrants received no such help. Black families that overcame the economic barriers to suburbanization faced backlash: in 1963, a mob of white Trotwood residents pelted a newly arrived black family with rocks when they dared to move into the neighborhood, shouting "two, four, six, eight, run the n****rs out of state!" By the 1960s, ninety-six percent of the Dayton metropolitan area's impoverished lived on the west side, and the city became the tenth most-segregated in the United States.

When Don L. Crawford—Dayton's first black city commissioner—presented Dr. Martin Luther King Jr. with a key to the city before a crowd at the University of Dayton in 1964, he warned King that it would not open homes on many streets and neighborhoods in the city. It was this lack of opportunity, this discrimination, this disenfranchisement that led the west side to rise up in resistance during the first "long hot summer" of 1966. Lyndon B. Johnson came to the Montgomery County Fair to try to calm things down, but another uprising occurred the following year. Dayton's were the earliest riots studied by the federal Kerner Commission, which reported that the city's black population were the least satisfied citizens of any major city with their income, education, and housing.

I discussed all of this with late historian Dr. Joseph Watras at Press Coffee in the Oregon District that fall, not far from his office at the University of Dayton. "Yes, redlining and restrictive covenants segregated Dayton," he acknowledged. "But the real story here is why Dayton *remained* segregated after we undertook that housing integration plan during the 1970s." My curiosity was piqued, and I made another trip to the *Dayton Daily News* Archive at Wright State University.

People knew the status quo could not hold in the wake of the uprisings of the 1960s. In September 1967, presidential hopeful George Romney's campaign conducted interviews on the west side to see how people were feeling about their lot in life. How could his campaign address the desperation of black Americans? One west side woman told a staffer about her and others' grassroots efforts to get a fair housing ordinance passed which would allow black Daytonians to move east of the Great Miami River and to the suburbs. To her, the problem was that west-siders were constrained within their poor neighborhoods. The city had to "break up the ghetto" and increase affordable housing in East Dayton and the suburbs in order to avoid more unrest. Romney listened.

And so did Dayton's business elite. Suburban whites were now afraid to come downtown to shop, and the national spotlight had shamed city leadership. The chief executives of National Cash Register, Frigidaire, General Motors, McCall's Printing, Dayton Tire, and others took this shame personally: one local described greater Dayton in the late 1960s as "a very large company town with enlightened paternalistic business leadership." The business elite called the shots in Dayton, and once the riots convinced them that racial segregation was bad for business, they organized to address it.

National Cash Register (NCR) organized a retreat at its suburban headquarters in the spring of 1968. CEOs and members of the Miami Valley Regional Planning Commission (MVRPC) agreed that the stock of affordable housing for poor black west-siders had to be increased in both East Dayton (predominantly Appalachian white) and in the suburbs (ninety-seven percent white). This business influence in urban planning had precedence in Dayton. John Patterson of NCR had advocated for the creation of the nation's first regional watershed district in the aftermath of the 1913 flood—which gave Arthur Morgan the chance to cut his teeth before heading up the Tennessee Valley Authority. Business elites, worried about corruption, made Dayton the country's first large city manager-run town, eschewing the mayoral-council system by the 1920s. Public servants had done the bidding of business for decades.

At the retreat, the Fair Share Housing Plan was born. Over the course of five years the MVRPC would generate 14,000 units of affordable housing in the suburbs of Dayton with the idea that poor black Daytonians would move into them. At the time, ninety-five percent of the region's subsidized housing lay within the limits of the City of Dayton. The plan would change that. The suburbs would finally be asked to contribute their "fair share" to the cause of increasing opportunity for the inner city's poor and disenfranchised—to take on their "fair share" of affordable housing. The business community enlisted the help of local homebuilders and construction companies to tout the plan while donating millions of private dollars to jumpstart the program. The Department of Housing and Urban Development (HUD) under George Romney, recently appointed to the position by President Richard Nixon, pledged units to MVRPC as well. HUD was itself pursuing a program of "opening the suburbs" as a part of the national response to the riots of the late 1960s.

Before building could start, however, the MVRPC had to convince suburbanites to allow the construction of federally subsidized housing in their backyards. This was no easy feat and suburban recalcitrance was marked. But as planners took the plan on the road during the summer of 1969, touring the school gymnasiums of the Miami Valley, they began to break through. One planner remembered that:

> "We went through a difficult–no, a hellish–summer. At some of the hearings the police were put on notice to escort staff in and out of town. Community members recited the Constitution, and the John Birch Society caused no end of trouble ... several racist organizations such as the John Birch Society, the Committee to Restore the Constitution, and the Ku Klux Klan, fought the plan. They were easy to deal with because their members could be baited at public hearings. When making presentations and answering questions, we would attempt to say things that would irritate these people. They would invariably respond with racist statements that would disgust the uncommitted people who didn't know a great deal about the issue or were undecided, but wouldn't identify with racists."

The business elite mobilized their friends at the *Dayton Daily News* and the *Dayton Journal Herald* in a public relations campaign to convince suburbanites that building affordable housing in the suburbs was the moral thing to do. Jim Fain, a civil rights reporter and editor of the *Daily News*, commissioned cartoons portraying lily-white Moraine as a "Dixie Suburb" and well-heeled Oakwood as a compound for the rich.

The more diverse suburbs of Jefferson Township, Trotwood, and Riverside were the first to fulfil their quota for affordable housing units in the early 1970s. Romney's HUD added to this early momentum by making the Fair Share Plan a national model by paying for Dayton planners to present their ideas in Washington, New York, and other large cities. Dayton became a "mecca for planners" interested in integrating the suburbs. By 1976, all suburbs except Oakwood and Moraine had built subsidized housing under the plan. However, the plan lost federal support after Nixon sacked Romney and his plan to open the suburbs to shore up his white suburban base. Even though suburban resistance to the Dayton plan stifled its success, by 1980 the City of Dayton had increased its subsidized housing units by seventy-four percent and the suburbs by 1,876 percent.

Yet during the 1970s, Dayton's suburbs gained only two percent in black population—and Dayton's became the third most-segregated major metropolitan area in the nation behind Cleveland and Chicago. West Dayton saw no more major uprisings, construction companies gained generous government contracts, and business elites maintained their control over the region's politics. But most black Daytonians remained segregated on the west side, in Jefferson Township, and in adjoining Trotwood (which flipped from majority white to majority black). The death of the Great Society, deindustrialization, and the importance of community were the major reasons that the plan did not lead to the residential racial integration of the metro area. Around the mid-1970s, Washington stopped funding newly constructed low-rent housing and switched instead to a form of subsidized housing which would come to be known as Section 8. Under this scheme, private owners would receive vouchers for low-income renters, and rents in these units were higher than those under the previous subsidized housing regime.

This might not have been an obstacle to prospective black suburbanites in 1970. Then, owing to good manufacturing jobs, West Dayton's average family income was around thirty percent higher than the national black average and was roughly on par with the white family national average. But because Dayton's business elites began moving their factories away from the metro to other cities, black Daytonians began to suffer disproportionately from deindustrialization as the decade wore on. Service jobs replaced well-paying ones. By 1980, the average West Dayton family income was only three percent higher than the national black average and was a whopping forty-five percent lower than the white family national average income. Because of the shift toward Section 8 and the loss of good jobs, by 1980 forty-eight percent of West Daytonians made *too little* to qualify for MVRPC units in the suburbs. Twenty-one percent of Daytonians now lived in poverty, up from fourteen percent in 1970.

In this climate of austerity, it is little wonder that average West Daytonians chose to remain close to their friends and relatives rather than suffer the slings and arrows of moving to a new neighborhood which lacked public transport and lacked not for prejudice. In West Dayton, relatives could provide childcare and mutual aid to compensate for the loss in wages that average black families suffered during the 1970s. Neighbors became even more important than ever. So, people stayed put. And it was East Daytonians and lower-income suburbanites who moved into the new suburban subsidized housing. Meanwhile, as black communities suffered from the shift to the information economy and a resurgent rightward turn in national politics, the white suburbs blossomed. Eventually, the construction of I-675 completely bypassed the City of Dayton as white, affluent exurbs came to constitute most of the metro's economic growth.

And so, the Fair Share plan didn't really change much. The federal government gave up on integrating American cities. The rich got richer, and the poor poorer. People moved less. Bubbles within bubbles formed as suburbs gave way to McMansion exurbs. And John Crawford lost his life.

The kind of fear of the "other" that was on display at those MVRPC meetings, in Trotwood when a new black family moved in: I think that that fears that affluent white suburbs foster breeds the kind of thinking that killed Crawford.

A few months into writing my master's thesis on the Fair Share plan, I heard a news story about a Starbucks in Philadelphia. The manager (a white woman) had called the police on a couple of friends (black) who were waiting for some other friends and were otherwise minding their own business. Where had she grown up? Her parents' place on the east side of Dayton.

Dayton's Voice: A Brief Personal History of Dayton City Paper

AMANDA DEE

My time as editor-in-chief of *Dayton City Paper* formally started with a gentleman's agreement in The Pine Club, a steakhouse that has earned its name from its pine-paneled walls and national accolades from its dry-aged cuts. The Pine Club menu hasn't changed since it was established in 1947 and, I suspect, neither has the core clientele of supper club regulars. Like the surrounding city, The Pine Club has become a monument to a bygone era of the industrial Midwest, when the region was a sphere of influence. When it mattered not only to the people who call it home. I was told I had to try the famous Pine Club stewed tomatoes—had to, in the way orders can pose as recommendations.

The bite of tomatoes tasted saccharine like a souvenir candy.

Across from me in the booth, Paul would laugh, "It's a handshake of course." His steak pooled like pink gasoline on the plate. He had been publisher of the *Dayton City Paper* since 2009 and owner since 2012, after other owners and iterations of the alt weekly, starting in 1993 as *The Dayton Voice*.

After I shook on it, I would learn how to negotiate his loud voice with quieter ones, which at times meant my own. Now, though, I would consider my options, or lack thereof. I'm a journalist in 2016. I am twenty-one, a few weeks shy of being a University of Dayton alumna. And like the restaurant and the city where I'm shaking on the next year and a half of my life; I don't believe this could have happened anywhere else.

The Pet Issue: August 2, 2016

At a weekly paper with a full-time staff that fluctuated around five, a theme issue was what Paul called a "hack" to secure a week of vacation time. When you don't have resources, you have to hack. And I was a full-time editorial department of one.

Every week we ran a group of local columnists, one of whom, Marc, had worked for about forty years at the *Dayton Daily News* on the sports beat. When I announced the timing of the year's annual Pet Issue to the writers, he warned me he was new to writing about pets. He then called after he finished his piece to warn me again: his column was a controversial one. About a former colleague who had eaten dog while covering the 1988 Seoul Olympics. Twice removed from the dog-eating and in the context of a culture where dog is part of the cuisine, I didn't see any reason to cut the piece. Maybe I should have.

We had also placed an ad for a no-kill animal shelter's fundraising dinner on the same page as Marc's dog-eating column.

We learned of our mistake after we had gone to print. Deep laughter burst from me. I was too tired to make it from my loveseat to my mattress most nights. And sometimes, there are mistakes and no hack. The paper and the city didn't survive on inventiveness alone, but also by grit, that laughter through pain that has stayed in my lungs even after leaving. The acceptance of what's gone wrong.

The Death Issue: October 25, 2016

I conceived The Death Issue to be my lasting mark on the paper. An all-black-printed, headline-less cover in the style of AC/DC's *Back In Black*. Dayton has a thing for metal. One of my most loyal writers performed as Ozzy Osbourne in a cover band. Our distribution team may have dreamed of strangling me with their black-inked fingers, but they had to have felt cool.

While the Death Issue was still on stands, our dining critic Paula found manx cats in a dumpster in historic Germantown, where spaying cats is not yet in fashion. I took in two, with black coats and nubs for tails like rabbits. They weighed in at a couple pounds, both crawling with fleas on the outside; one with worms on the inside, which soon became outside and onto the shag carpet of my one-bedroom in Grafton Hills, where I was living alone for the first time.

I hesitated before taking them in, worried about taking in cats, worried about caring for two alone on my schedule. But on the loveseat that had become a bed, the cats filled in the spaces, and others.

Dayton Skyscrapers: December 13, 2016

I visited Willis Bing Davis's art studio on Third Street, a few addresses north of the river on the and a few minutes from my Grafton Hill apartment. His studio is wallpapered with art and mementos from Davis's life and the lives of artists he cares about or taught. We talked about "Dayton Skyscrapers," an art project that spotlights black community members throughout the city's history.

When we published the coverage at the paper with an error, he offered me gratitude for featuring the project. I offered him an in-person apology.

I think back to a year earlier, at the student newspaper, how I equated apologizing to an admittance of blame, which I equated to a journalistic faux pas. I wonder if this is what we are taught in journalism school or everywhere. Now what are journalists, more strapped by their limited resources, instructed about apologies? About living with a community? I hope we are teaching to apologize, to acknowledge when we make mistakes, to recognize the limitations we and our communities face.

Surviving Brock Turners: January 10, 2017

If you google "Abertooth Lincoln," you will likely see a photo of the punk band's lead singer burning a copy of my cover story. The cover, convicted sex offender and former Oakwood resident Brock Turner, is a stand-in, a name and face associated with lenient punishment for sexual assault on college campuses. You will likely see how some of Dayton screams back in the face of injustice.

A year after I left the *Dayton City Paper*, on Tuesday, September 18, 2018, my old recurring nightmare came true: the paper didn't come out. I read the news from the distance of another, larger city and watched as my stories, my writers' stories, Dayton's stories, turned into a closed archive, another document of the city's history.

The End of 105.9 WNKU

MATTHEW SZOZDA

There is a mystery hidden in this Midwest sound,
Wrapped in sovereign songs.
The kind of magic you wear with windows down on I-75.
Left-hand riding the waves of a thin wind.

Now, a countdown of days until your last broadcast.
When we heard the news,
The city stopped and bathed in its own frequency,
In this place we know all sweet things must expire.

We hold them with a heavy inhale,
And press them out of our chests once we've used them dry.
We hope they return to us full again.
And is this not the recipe for great American songs?

Born in a thin wind returned from our mouths,
In a fleeting sound too poor to sing another note.

My Journey in the Land of Funk: From Rochester, New York, to Dayton, Ohio

SCOT BROWN

Leroy "Sugarfoot" Bonner—the iconic lead singer and guitarist of the Ohio Players—was in no mood to talk to some dude from out of town researching the 1970s heyday of Dayton, Ohio's reign as a hotbed of soul and funk music. "Sugar" or "Foots," as he was called, had to be nudged into it. But who in the Gem City had the gravitas to urge this deeply philosophical—sometimes moody—and always brilliant funk legend to talk to me?

I had practically given up on the idea until I met Samie and Earl Reid, who fronted The Reid Brothers band—a fraternal blues duo known for flashy guitar play, bedazzling on-stage antics, cowboy-like gun-slinging, and boundless generosity toward younger musicians. The two had migrated to Ohio from Georgia in the late 1950s. When I met them in July of 2007, they were among the few legends still living in Dayton for whom Sugarfoot had unqualified respect.

"You need to talk to this man who came all the way from California," Samie told Sugarfoot after a few minutes of phone banter and catching up. Sugarfoot conceded! I jumped into the rental car and dipped out of the west Dayton area, speeding cautiously over to neighboring Trotwood just a few minutes away.

Sugarfoot had every reason to avoid wasting time. That summer, after recovering from a major health setback while on the road with the Ohio Players, he began steadfastly working toward making a musical comeback with a new band of his own called Sugarfoot's Ohio Players. After being escorted in, I found Sugarfoot seated in front of a keyboard in his home studio. However, before I could begin the interview, he took on an interrogative tone of his own.

"Let me ask you a question, do you play any instruments yourself?"

With the hope of getting the chance to jam with any number of my musical idols, I had brought my bass guitar along with me on this research trip.

"I do. I actually play bass, and it's in the trunk," I responded.

"Go get it," he insisted.

Once I plugged up, Sugarfoot asked, "Can you play *Skin Tight?*", then ran through the main groove and bridge with me, and proceeded to give me a lesson on playing the blues. The tutorial ended with him advising me to "keep practicing."

By 2007, when I conducted the interview, I was already a couple of years deep into studying the history of the Dayton music scene. As the project sauntered along, I began to hear numerous stories of young musicians in the 1960s and 70s who received informal lessons from experienced musicians like Sugarfoot. They would share their knowledge of music making with eager novices looking to learn. This community-based example of arts education constitutes just one of the many facets in an extensive local music culture and tradition that contributed to Dayton's emergence as an urban funk haven.

The notion of receiving a blues lesson from a funk icon speaks to the eclectic roots of a genre born of intersecting and pre-existing traditions in African American music—gospel, blues, jazz, rhythm and blues, soul, rock, and anything in between. This infectious danceable style emphasizes rhythm and a set of sound relationships known as 'the groove.'

Funk is obviously more than a four-letter word; it is a musical style that reached a peak in commercial popularity during the 1970s through the mid 1980s. While the term "funk" did not garner official sanction as a chart category in *Billboard* magazine, numerous musicians either explicitly identified as funk artists or described their music as "funk," or at the very least, "funky."

Like most musical styles, the distinction between funk and other genres is neither fixed nor consistent. Historians have located linguistic roots to "funky" as a reference to unpleasant odors in Central African languages. "Funk" or "funky" appears—as a description or category of sound and evocative feeling—in vernacular characterizations of blues, ragtime, early jazz, and other popular music styles.

In the late 1960s and early 70s, James Brown, Sly & the Family Stone, The Ohio Players and Parliament/Funkadelic made foundational contributions to the making of the funk music genre. Building on the styles and commercial success of these trendsetters, a myriad of self-contained bands followed up by adding their own stamp to the genre, including Earth, Wind & Fire, Pleasure, Graham Central Station, Rufus featuring Chaka Khan, The Bar-Kays, Con Funk Shun, Rick James and

The Stone City Band, Mother's Finest, The Brothers Johnson, Cameo, and many others.

This journey through Dayton, Ohio, surveys its historic standing as an epicenter of funk and a haven of Black self-contained bands during the 1970s and early 80s. My interest in the subject is the outcome of growing up and being introduced to musical instruments and bands in Rochester, New York, a city very much like Dayton, which shares a heritage of having once been ripe with manufacturing jobs. Beyond this connection, I have no tribal links to the Gem City beyond a great admiration for the music it birthed.

My book on Dayton funk is not a tale itself but is filled with them— tales that came together to create the people and the conditions which made Dayton—a city in which African Americans comprised over one-third of a population of a medium-sized city—the home of the largest per capita number of funk bands signed to major record labels during the 1970s: The Ohio Players (Westbound and Mercury), Slave (Cotillion/Atlantic), Steve Arrington's Hall of Fame (Atlantic), Lakeside (SOLAR), Roger and Zapp (Warner Bros.), Sun (Capitol), Faze-O (S.H.E./Atlantic), Aurra (Dream Records and Salsoul), Platypus (Casablanca), Dayton (Liberty), Shadow (Elektra), Junie (Westbound and CBS) and Heatwave (Epic).

Funk music and Black bands are not synonymous but are very closely connected, especially at the local level. Bands were the dominant unit of artistic expression in the golden age of funk. To unpack and examine the two and their interconnectedness—from the ground up—requires one to roll around in the urban socioeconomic and cultural soil from which Black bands were born.

Dayton's special contribution to the development of funk as a popular style during the 1970s is a history that raises questions beyond the beats, the sounds and the notes, or artist biographies. What was the relationship between this local music tradition and changing socioeconomic conditions in the late 1960s through the 1980s? How was this local scene tied to the social and cultural politics of race and space in a segregated city? How did the wave of Dayton bands, contracted with major record labels, fit into the larger music industry trends in the 1970s? Why did Black bands—and by extension, Dayton funk groups—decline as an artistic unit in popular music? The answers require an engagement with the 'everyday people' and institutional actors involved in the circulation of funk music within this urban community (youth, parents, teachers, public schools, churches, record stores, managers, disc jockeys, radio stations, recreation centers, recording studios, and vinyl pressing plants), and the dynamics of race and power at the macro level of the music industry.

The experience of Dayton bands underscores the complicated two-way exchange between music as a part of a local cultural economy and its widened commodified form in the popular music marketplace. On the one hand, the sonic formula of funk bands (groove-centered instrumentation and soulful vocal arrangements) was not only the result of commercial trends determined by record companies or from the 'top' and 'down' to consumers. Typically, funk band members initially developed their craft and approaches to music in urban communities and public spheres anchored in Black working class social and cultural scenes. The recorded sound of bands was often shaped by artistic treks from basement rehearsals to performances at school talent shows, then from there on to local nightclubs and multiple spaces in Black public spheres.

The connection between popular funk sounds and undergirding sociologies of urban communities is not limited to specific cities or regions. The role of community institutions is an under-recognized but consistent theme in the music histories of funk luminaries, including James Brown and networks of local Black clubs and performance venues ('the chitlin' circuit'); Sly & The Family Stone and Black Pentecostal church and Bay Area countercultural movements; The Ohio Players and nightclubs in the Tri-State region (Ohio, Indiana and Kentucky), Parliament/Funkadelic and Black barber shops in Plainfield and Newark, New Jersey; War and youth "low-rider" car culture in Los Angeles; and even Rick James and Prince and the music education in public schools in Buffalo and Minneapolis, respectively.

Funk-Storiography

Writing about funk as a historian doesn't yet feel as natural as the body movements that funk is known to induce. This scholarly stiffness may very well be a momentary cramp in style, as major strides toward historicizing funk have moved steadily forward in recent decades. Aware that funk was in the rearview as a commercially dominant strain in popular music, Rickey Vincent began his tenure as a Bay Area disc jockey in the 1980s, and was committed to preserving the funk tradition and supporting veteran funk artists who struggled for access to the airwaves. He went on to pen *Funk: The Music, the People, and the Rhythm of the One* (1996), which endures as an interdisciplinary and foundational overview of funk. Studies of funk by scholars of musicology, ethnomusicology, history, cultural studies, literature, as well as first-person accounts in autobiographies thereafter would add more detail and specificity to specific artists, geographies, regions, and compositions. Funk, like blues, jazz, and, more recently, hip-hop, has inspired scholarly production from multiple disciplinary standpoints. "Funk" and "funkiness" are fertile grounds for theorizing about broad aspects of the human experience, including freedom of expression, conformity, environmental sustainability, political rebellion, social stratification, respectability politics, the construction of gender roles, sexuality, and sexual expression.

Commentary and lyrics by musicians themselves stand out as important interventions in thinking about funk from a philosophical perspective, especially since many sought to define their own funk strain; "P-Funk" (Parliament/Funkadelic), "C on the Funk" (Cameo), "Gentlemen's Funk" (GQ), "Punk Funk" (Rick James), and "Sophistafunk" (James Mtume and Reggie Lucas). James Brown and Parliament/Funkadelic offered a trove of concepts to facilitate the construction of ideational propositions. In *Funk,* Vincent also evoked James Brown's technique of structuring instrumentation to emphasize music's first beat of a 4/4 time signature (called "the one") as a framework for describing a funk ethos of unity that also includes and encourages individual freedom. He also examined the philosophy of P-Funk and cited one of the early scholarly theses on the subject, *The P-Funk Aesthetic* by Michael O'Neal.

A decade after *Funk* was initially published, a symposium called "Eruptions of Funk" brought together cultural theorists, historians, musicologists, and writers with research and creative interests in funk. Organized by Tony Bolden, the event inspired an edited collection of essays on funk and helped ignite his editorship of the *American Studies Journal's* special edition dedicated to funk. The elasticity and iconoclastic character of the term "funk" in its vernacular form, lends itself to a variety of uses as a baseline concept in the development of cutting-edge social and cultural theory.

Expanded explorations of funk philosophies coincided with an interest in regionally specific styles and histories. In 1997, Vincent consulted for an exhibition at the National Afro-American Museum and Cultural Center (NAMCC) in Wilberforce, Ohio: "Something in the Water: The Sweet Sound of Dayton Street Funk" organized by visionary NAMCC curator, Michael Sampson, and renowned ethnomusicologist, Portia Maultsby, director of the Archives of African American Music and Culture at Indiana University. Maultsby's 2001 article, "Funk Music: An Expression of Black Life in Dayton, Ohio and the American Metropolis," was a pioneering look at Dayton funk. In addition, independent memoirs written by John "Turk" Logan, former program director of Dayton's WDAO radio station, and another personal reflection by Greg Webster, drummer for the Ohio Players during the late '60s and early '70s, represent significant steps toward documenting the history of Dayton's unique place in Black music history.

While my upcoming book, tentatively entitled, *Tales from the Land of Funk,* follows a trail blazed by earlier works, this funk story re-imagines the concept of arts education and highlights the centrality of relationships between teachers and Black students, and the Black public sphere and bands. Nearly all the members of the funk and R&B bands from Dayton, as well as those from other cities, received extensive musical training from public schools and mentorship from older musicians. The story of Dayton funk exposes the cultural consequences of arts education and operative functioning beyond the classroom. Relationships between teachers and students in Dayton's predominantly Black schools were fundamental to the growth and training of youth bands. These tales highlight organic models of arts education based on shared spaces and places where people congregated and lived: 1) teachers and students in Dayton established a model of arts education based on extensive civic engagement; 2) residential proximity was an important context for the social and pedagogical interrelationships between students, teachers, and the schools; and 3) older musicians were important mentors and teachers of younger musicians in this community-based pedagogy and often worked in partnership with formal music instructors.

Dayton's teachers, students, talent shows, and nightclubs, have homes on wax. Long rehearsal hours can explain the production of exceptionally tight and complex compositional arrangements in recordings. Dayton bands were also known to codify a community-based performance aesthetic explicitly in their songs: Ohio Players' "Introducing the Ohio Players" (1975), Lakeside's "All the Way Live" (1978), "Fantastic Voyage" (1980), and "Ain't No Half Steppin" (1976), Slave's "Stone Jam" (1980), Sun's "Sun Is Here" (1978), Roger's "Do It Roger" (1981), Zapp's "Brand New Player" (1980), and Junie's "Super J" (1975). These songs embody the spirit live of performance—lyrically affirming the artists' ability to move the crowd to beats and instrumental arrangements that sound like jam sessions or the opening of a concert.

Understanding the story of Dayton funk opens the ear to the story of a community in sound. The sonic calculus perfected by James Brown, Sly Stone, and '70s funk bands is a force shaped by the historic struggle for Black communities in multiple contexts. Even small slices of songs contain the vision, labor, creativity and struggle of the "everyday people" who made the Gem City a veritable "land of funk."

LOVE
LETTERS

Dayton Took a Chance on Me

NAN WHALEY

In 1994, I decided to cross the state line from Indiana to attend the University of Dayton. I knew one person, my roommate, who went to the same high school. Like any college freshman, I felt the fear and excitement of moving somewhere new. What I didn't expect was how much I would fall in love with this new city.

When I decided to go to a school in Ohio, my parents were not exactly thrilled. I think they always thought I would stay close by and go to Indiana University. They didn't know much about Ohio, but, as staunch, active Democrats, they knew it nearly always decided who would be the president. They also knew, and reminded me, that I was able to go to UD because of policies from President Bill Clinton that expanded access to higher education. Their one requirement was that I get involved in politics, so I volunteered on his reelection campaign. I dutifully took the RTA bus from campus down to the old Democratic headquarters on Wilkinson Street.

I had grown up in a small town in Indiana, the sort of town where families had been there for generations. It wasn't a place that would feel welcoming to an outsider. Dayton was the opposite. From the moment I showed up on campus and at Democratic headquarters, I found a community that would open itself up to me.

I felt belonging. I felt like I was home.

After college, I chose to stay in Dayton. As I got more and more involved in the community, I eventually decided to run for Dayton City Commission. So at the age of 29, I ran citywide for an open seat. I was a young, single woman. I didn't own a house. I had absolutely no relatives in Dayton or the area. What did the people of Dayton do? They elected me—an outsider—anyway. They gave me a chance.

There is a lot to love about Dayton. It is a place that reinvents itself over and over again. No matter what comes our way: floods, tornadoes, or gun violence, we stand firm together and fight back. I love that we are resilient. I love our grit.

But what I love most about our city is that we are welcoming. No matter where you come from, what you believe, or who you love; you are welcome here. Dayton took a chance on me, as it has on so many other people who have chosen to call this place home.

Origins

ANNETTE CHAVEZ

I have often wondered why people end up practicing medicine in a place such as Dayton, Ohio. It is my hometown and I have never considered leaving my family, friends, and comfortable life here. But if you page through our county medical society physician directory you find that Dayton is a virtual United Nations of medicine. Listed are doctors who graduated from medical schools in Canada, Egypt, Bolivia, Pakistan, India, Turkey, Hungary, Iran, Ghana, and multiple other countries around the globe.

How did they all end up here? I am certain every physician has an excellent reason to call our humble Midwestern city their home and to treat the citizens here as their patients. Some live here for the job opportunities for their spouse or their ties to Wright-Patterson Air Force Base. Certainly serendipity may play a role in bringing physicians to Dayton. I thought I would tell you why I am here.

I have a Spanish surname and yes, I kept my maiden name. One might think my family immigrated from Cuba when Castro came to power. Or maybe I am descended from Mexican migrant farmworkers who were able to make a better life for their children in the U.S. Or you might suppose my parents were both physicians educated in Peru who came to the U.S. to flee the civil unrest caused by the Shining Path guerillas.

Actually, my parents were born in Colorado. Our ancestors came to the New World in 1598 with Don Juan de Onate, prior to the arrival of the Pilgrims on the Mayflower. My parents grew up in a bilingual community in the San Luis Valley of Colorado and followed many of the old Spanish traditions. My grandparents were addressed as "Don" and "Dona" and celebrated all of the Catholic feast days such as Santiago and May Crownings. However, there is evidence that they and many of the other inhabitants of the Southwest were actually descendants of Sephardic Jews who were forced to convert to Catholicism after the Moors were driven from Spain. I am not certain of my family's Jewish heritage but my father was named Simon and I had an Uncle Solomon and an Uncle Levi.

So why did my Spanish-speaking parents leave their families and tight-knit community to spend the rest of their lives in Dayton? They often spoke of the discrimination that they experienced when they ventured outside of their hometowns and were determined that their children would not share the same treatment. My mother relates the story of getting a "C" in Spanish class in college even though she was fluent in the language taught by the parish priests (who hailed from Spain). A non-fluent non-Hispanic classmate of mom's with poor command of Spanish was awarded an "A" in the same class.

My father was drafted into the Army during World War II and was commissioned a Second Lieutenant after completing Officer Candidate School. He stayed at that rank, passed over for promotion, until he separated from the military when the war ended. My mom and dad cringed when people commented on their accents, so they decided not to teach their children Spanish so there would be no evidence that we were anything but "American." But the worst indignity was to be labeled and treated as "dirty Mexicans," and this fueled my father's efforts to escape the West with its beautiful mountains and prejudice. After the war my father earned his master's degree and then a PhD in education from the University of Colorado. He had a wife and two daughters by then but he could not find an academic position. His doctoral advisor gave him some classes to teach at CU but he needed a full-time salary to support his family. He picked up some odd jobs, working on a road crew laying asphalt and then in construction blowing insulation into houses. He was mortified when a student of his saw him covered in insulation on a sweaty day and exclaimed "Dr. Chavez? Is that you?" It was a job, but not what he was educated to do. After some time searching, my father became desperate for a teaching position. He sent resumes everywhere. Mom bought produce by the bushel and spent her summer canning it so they could have food in the winter. Their parents were not well off and could not provide financial support.

Facing lean times caused my parents to intensify their prayers. They said the rosary, novenas, and lit candles in church. They attended mass and prayed to the Blessed Virgin Mary. Dad's PhD advisor contacted colleagues around the country to inquire about any openings on their faculty. For a long time there was nothing. Finally, on the feast day of the Immaculate Conception (December 8), Dad was offered a position with the U.S. Army as an education specialist in Florida. My parents were so grateful they said tearful prayers of thanksgiving at mass that day. They packed up their small children and belongings and moved to West Palm Beach. The job paid well and Dad stayed at it for a year before he remembered that he didn't much care for the military, even though he was a civilian. He started his search once again for a faculty position at a university.

He discovered that there was an institution in the Midwest run by an order of priests and brothers who were dedicated to the Blessed Virgin Mary. In fact, they were called "Marianists." Dad had never heard of that order. The Spanish priests back home were Theatines, and he had known of Jesuits and Franciscans. It had to be a sign. Had they not been devoted to Mary, prayed to her for a job, and received one on her feast day? And now there was a position at a "Marianist" university. Dad interviewed and was offered the position at a significantly reduced pay level from what he was earning with the army. No matter. The family moved to a city in Ohio that they had barely heard of, which was home to the University of Dayton. Dad became a professor of elementary education and eventually served as department chair. In the apex of his career Dad's elementary ed department was named one of five outstanding colleges of teacher education in the country. My father was a humble man but was immensely proud of that achievement. He was innovative well beyond his time in training elementary school teachers. He published scholarly articles, mentored PhD students, and was a favorite of his undergraduate students.

Once in Dayton, Mom and Dad had three more children delivered by our family doctor at St. Elizabeth Hospital. I was number four of five. We never left Dayton. This was the only home I ever knew. Our family did take regular epic cross-country treks in the old tan station wagon with the luggage in the roof rack. We arrived at Grandma and Grandpa's after three days and played with our cousins in the ice-cold Culebra River, climbed the foothills, and explored Grandpa's ranch. Then we returned to Ohio with a funny Spanglish accent that took about a week to wear off.

My parents wanted a better life for us in Dayton, and we were blessed in many ways. I was raised in the very non-diverse suburb of Kettering and never experienced any prejudice. My friends all had German surnames and I grew up with the Cincinnati Reds and UD basketball. At one point my dad was offered a job at Northwestern University for double the pay of what he earned at UD. But the family had grown roots here and was thriving. All five of us earned graduate degrees and served in good careers. And one of us even became a physician, a first in a family of teachers. That nearly free education at the University of Dayton for all of us was certainly crucial.

My cousins in Colorado didn't all fare as well. I do have two other physician cousins as well as a few who are engineers, lawyers, and nurses. There are a ton of teachers, of course. But others have struggled, although it may not have anything to do with being raised in a poor, isolated community.

In my nuclear family we had the advantage of a fresh start, a quality education, and two really excellent parents.

When I was in the eighth grade, my father was invited back to his undergraduate alma mater, Adams State College, to give the commencement address. He was quite honored to speak to the students, two of whom were his nephews, and worked very diligently on his speech. He quoted the Spanish poet Federico Garcia Lorca and spoke to the students of serving the poor, especially addressing the plight of migrant farm workers.

My parents missed their family "back home" but grew to love Dayton and became part of the community. Here there was no Las Posadas but there were UD football games, croquet in the backyard and fifty baby boomer children on the same cul-de-sac to play with us kids. I couldn't have asked for a better childhood and after I was a UD Flyer I became an Ohio State Buckeye, a St. Elizabethan, and have since remained a lifelong Daytonian. My father is buried in Calvary Cemetery just a few blocks away from my family practice office in Kettering. I have several patients who are retired teachers who happened to have had my dad as their professor at UD. Before my mother entered the twilight of her years with dementia, she often accompanied me to the Salud free clinic for migrant workers and translated for me as I treated the patients.

Dayton is my home and I will remain forever grateful to my parents for leaving everything that was familiar to them to come to a strange, flat, green part of the country to raise us. I will continue to count the citizens of the Dayton area as my patients for the rest of my career, all because of the Blessed Virgin Mary, the University of Dayton, my parents' enduring faith, and the power of prayer.

Previously published in Dayton Medicine, The Journal of the Montgomery County Medical Society, *Oct/Nov 2013 issue.*

The Spot By The Side Of The Road, Woodman Fen

RON KNIPFER

It's not like its surrounding
a drop of nature 'mid city's pounding.
There's not a bird that couldn't be heard
or wouldn't be welcome with open arms
in this sanctuary with ancient charms.

The right time of year you may get a chance
to watch mayflies dance among water plants
or pollywogs sun on old oak logs
or gentle winds blow 'cross winter snow.

With its sylvan history woven in mystery
I hear it call: "Come walk my corridors."

Author's note: The Woodman Fen is a natural area administered by Five Rivers MetroParks and is located near the intersection of Woodman and Patterson streets in Dayton. This poem was read at the anniversary meeting of Five Rivers MetroParks in 2013.

The Gift in the Parking Lot of John Hole Elementary for my Stepson

ERICA MANTO-PAULSON

The vampire cartoon drawing
that said "I love you more
than all the flowers"
on what would be the last day
he would ever run towards me
after school, flinging himself
at me like a wild dragon—
all wide eyed
and fire breathing
while the other children
walked to their parents
in the ordinary way.
Catching him, barely
again, I laughed and said
you're getting too big
and pulling me in
like a secret he whispered
you still catch me—
breathing in my scent,
waving the vampire drawing
in his hand
like a banner.

Paper Cut

HAYLEY SNYDER

It was Father's Day, and mine was in an ambulance. Barreling down the cracks of Route 22 toward Pittsburgh Presbyterian Hospital, and he was all alone. He faced a possible thumb amputation, of all things.

I set out on the four-hour stretch of highway that lay before me. I was still learning the scenery. The flat ground that spanned miles in every direction had been liberating at first. The shadows of Pennsylvania valleys had closed me in for too long. But whirring past acres of farmland as far as the eye could see, sparse trees pointed fingers at my loneliness.

I called my dad to tell him I was on my way, but he wasn't having it. I could barely hear his faraway voice, but it was telling me not to drive out in the dark.

And though the paper cut had turned his thumb black with infection, it would be saved, minus a few layers of skin.

I turned around at a gas station right off the highway. The summer downpour had since cleared the way for the golden sun to descend behind the Ohio landscape. With more room to spread, its rays shot further than I'd ever seen before. Behind me, the yellow mixed with black clouds. The storm was moving steadily east. God painted a message for me in the sky that night. And the message was this: Your dad is dying.

I had a brief spell of hopefulness when he was discharged from the hospital a few days later, although it didn't quite sit right with me.

He called me late that evening, and my most feared words came filtering through the phone in his gravelly voice: pancreatic cancer.

He didn't sound scared. He was the bravest person I knew.

I wanted to break down and scream, "I knew it all along!"

But instead I said, "Okay."

I wanted to be brave like him.

The following month would be a blur. I remember lying in bed while my husband stood at the foot of the bed staring at me with an expression that seemed a mixture of concern with a hint of disgust. He wanted to help me. He couldn't.

"I am the withering flower." I couldn't look at him.

"Okay, you can lay here, but all this doom and gloom all the time is too much." He left the room.

I remember watching him stir a pot of goulash. I watched the noodle and meat mixture get pushed back and forth, hissing with heat and throwing off mist.

"I think I'm in Purgatory," I said.

"What?" He hadn't taken his eyes off the skillet.

I knew that he heard me, but I repeated myself.

He said that *we* were going to get me through this.

I saw my father once more before the end. As I turned twenty-six, my eyes lingered on him as his lips mouthed the words to "Happy Birthday," but I'm not sure any sound came out. He was quiet, like me. Even in terminal sickness, he wanted no attention or sympathy.

And before we set out on the long drive back to Dayton, he uttered words that I couldn't believe he would need to confirm.

"Now you're all grown up, I hope I was a good dad."

My dad would live for twelve more days. It ended up being a heart attack that took him. A few people told me that was really a blessing, since he no longer had to suffer. I wanted to scream.

And after all arrangements had been made, after I'd spoken at his funeral, I found myself back in a city that I still felt like I didn't know.

My husband and I had barely been living in the Dayton area for a year, and we had hardly settled into our new townhouse in the city of West Carrollton.

We had no family in the city, not anywhere in Ohio. We had moved here to get out of our hometown. We knew it wasn't glamorous, but we had always wanted the experience of living somewhere different. We weren't very picky about where, and many people questioned our decision. *Why Dayton, of all places?* Truthfully, I really couldn't think of a great explanation. When my father got sick, I felt it was one of the biggest mistakes of my life.

I felt a sense of urgency to somehow make it all worth it. Even though we'd moved for jobs, we'd both switched jobs since the move.

We made a few friends. We'd talk about finding things to do around the city. Every time I drove past Bill's Donut Shop, I remembered my dad texting me about it, telling me that I should go there because it made the list of "Best Donut Shops in America." But I always just kept driving.

A cat café opened in Dayton that winter, and I asked my husband if he'd go with me. I felt a bit pathetic about it, but even that small trip for coffee felt like an adventure.

So many times I'd silently keep tally of why it was better to be here than there, desperately trying to make this city worth it. I'd enjoy occasional doses of laughter with a friend at work, or within the Dungeons and Dragons group we had recently formed. I'd drive on I-75 past the skyscrapers at sunset. At a certain moment, they looked like nothing more than papier-mâché, bathed in pink and gold. I'd admire the miles that I could see stretched out on either side on my commute to work. The way the wheat fields sometimes looked like paintings as they met with clouds on the clear horizon.

There was a Marathon gas station beside the apartment complex and friendly people who worked there. In time, I wouldn't have to ask for what I wanted. They'd have it ready before I reached the counter.

With all this discovery, a sense of loneliness persisted. Thoughts of my mother living alone stayed with me. The image of my dad decaying while I lived a state away was not fading.

And I think my husband had tried to help me, in his way. The only way he may have known. But sometimes there is no immediate solution to pain. And maybe he was growing tired of being patient. Maybe he saw me as a burden. Maybe *we* weren't going to get me through this.

When he left on that summer day, the sense of pointlessness washed over me once more, in a way it never had before. I had moved with this man, only for him to decide that he no longer wanted me to be part of his story. The terror of finding myself living alone in a city and state hours away from my family stiffened me, penetrated my bones. The dream of our life together faded in a matter of minutes. The townhouse felt like my tomb. Dayton felt like a curse on my life. And I was alone.

I became woozy from the enormity of my new world. And though others would tell me how free I now was to choose my new future, it wasn't freedom that I felt. It was more like my first time spinning a globe in grade school. Sometimes being in a big place does little more than remind you of how small you are.

I got lost on the way home from a friend's house in Huber Heights. I passed an apartment complex that my husband and I had toured once. The roads were empty at 3:00 a.m. I wondered how many others were out there like me. How many lost and abandoned. How many living on the fumes of anger.

I drove just to get my bearings on my new life in a still unknown land. Fatherless, husbandless, identities I still didn't understand. From the back roads of West Carrollton to the cobblestone streets of the Oregon District, my ringless hand shook as it turned my steering wheel of its own accord. My brain seemed to lack true power over my body. It was too preoccupied.

I renewed the lease at the townhouse. My townhouse. I rearranged the furniture. I packed away the dusty wedding vows that hung on the wall. I put pictures in boxes. I danced in the living room. I took walks around the complex at night. I cooked meals just for myself. I paid every bill. I learned to live alone.

But I wasn't alone. I found the Gem City to have a fitting name, as I met some of the truest people there. Someone to talk away the hours with so I wouldn't have to face reality for just a slice of the day. Someone to wade with me through the murky waters of grief. Someone to make me laugh. Someone to finally go with me to Bill's Donut Shop on a whim at 2:30 a.m.

The Gem City Catfé became a regular spot. Coffee and cats were staples in my life, reminders of the good things. On one particular evening I found myself discussing college football with someone who through circumstance, timing, and a connection I couldn't dismiss, I'd grown quite close to through the mess.

I didn't know much about football, but I did know that Ohio State's mascot was Brutus Buckeye. I just didn't realize that a buckeye was a nut. I thought it was a chocolate peanut butter cookie. Since moving to Ohio, I'd seen them at work potlucks and fudge shops. They were delicious.

His brown eyes crinkled in laughter.

"It's a nut from a buckeye tree. It's Ohio's state tree. See?" He held up his phone screen to educate me. And a far off memory surfaced almost as a lightbulb over my head.

A friend of mine had sent me one of those very nuts in the mail years ago. She said it was good luck to carry one with you. She thought I could use it. I didn't believe much in luck, but I put it in my purse where it never crossed my mind until my fingers would brush against it while searching for a pen or a lighter. But I was suddenly very aware of it as I sat rather comfortably in the Buckeye State. Like I was meant to be holding a maple turmeric coffee at that very moment, talking with this very man on East Fifth Street in Dayton, Ohio. I had carried that nut with me for years. Or perhaps it had somehow carried me.

I didn't know if it was good luck or bad luck or no luck at all that brought me to Southwest Ohio. If it was God's providence or fate or just the result of a bold choice that I made with a man I once loved enough to take such a risk with. Maybe it was as random as the paper cut on my dad's finger.

———————

But the Gem City forged a new woman out of the soul I thought I knew. Minerals of loss, love, abandonment, anger, hope, despair, grief, promise. They were pressed on all sides. They made it through. They made something new. She was as strong as the city she now called home.

Dayton, Ohio—A New Place to Call Home

BELINDA WRIGHT

Dayton, Ohio has been my home for over twenty years, but I still consider myself an outsider. Not that I have been made to feel that way—not in the least, but every now and then I still come across a native Daytonian who refers to landmarks and events that are obscure to me, while their memory is as fresh as yesterday.

I arrived in Dayton accompanying my husband on his new job assignment. Along with two small boys, we landed in West Dayton unaware of its history and challenges. We found a welcoming, close-knit community that embraced us warmly and offered us assistance as we settled in our new home and surroundings.

Within a few short years, the marriage took a turn for the worse and I was faced with the dilemma of finding another place to live. Dayton was still fairly new to me and I had no other family in the area. The people that I had met were "our" friends and "our" neighbors. My relationships with them had been as part of a couple or family, as someone's wife, someone's mom. When considering walking away from the marriage, I had to consider walking away from them as well.

While pondering these life-changing circumstances, I was confronted to look at Dayton with a new and different perspective. My introduction to Dayton was as an unemployed, stay-at-home mom with the security of a home and a provider. Three years later, I found myself having to find a place to live and a means of support for myself and possibly my sons (the arrangements for caring for the boys eventually led to a shared parenting agreement). Although I held an accounting degree, I had not worked for a number of years in the field and with the advancement in software and technology, I knew there were some challenges ahead to finding meaningful employment.

The idea of divorce was overwhelming in itself, particularly in a city where I had no roots. Still, I saw Dayton as a city to start over and re-define myself. I was also impressed by the many acquaintances I encountered who had left the area at one time and decided to return. Although they possessed the skills and talents to be successful any place, they chose to return to Dayton—to come home. That spoke volumes to me.

As I struggled to process and adjust to my new life, I knew I needed a place to start fresh, and since I was already here, Dayton became a feasible option. I decided not to move my sons far from their father. If possible, I thought it best that we live in the same city and since his job was here, I would try my best to settle here as well.

I soon found comfortable, affordable housing and those same friends and neighbors that I had come to know proved themselves to be not only great friends but my new adopted family. They helped me move to a new apartment and one even recommended me for an administrative position at United Theological Seminary. It was the love and generosity of my West Dayton family that confirmed my decision to stay. They took me in as a daughter, a sister, a best friend.

I have since found a number of opportunities in Dayton and feel my life has flourished here. I was able to go back to school and earn an advanced degree (kudos to Antioch University). I've held administrative positions at a seminary, a megachurch, and a start-up tech business. Currently, I work for a government subcontractor (Wright-Patterson Air Force Base is a driving force of employment opportunities).

I became a volunteer with the Victoria Theatre Association and have been exposed to theater and arts I had not imagined. I tried to soak in as many experiences as they had to offer, so much so that they offered me a job! Now I work there part-time with house management and crowd control. Outside of the VTA, Dayton has many art venues and organizations that are enriching and entertaining. Contrary to what one might think, there is plenty to do in Dayton!

Dayton is not a perfect city, but it offered the perfect opportunity for me to transform my life and learn to stand on my own. When asked "where are you from?", I still respond "Virginia," which is my birth state, but I'm quick to add, "but I live in Dayton!"

Tuesday's Child

JILL SUMMERVILLE

Look at the Dayton, Ohio, skyline, if you can. You must admit, that skyline has some worthy (some might even say, superior) competition nearby. Columbus, Ohio, which has over a dozen theaters in the downtown area alone, is just an hour away. That homage to mid-twentieth-century architecture, the Chicago skyline, is only four and a half hours away. Chicago's theaters can take some credit for that beauty; unlike most of Columbus', the downtown theaters of Chicago are big enough to have lights of their own that are part of the skyscape.

For the little amount of illumination it provides, the Dayton skyline's glow takes much effort to maintain. The skyline *is* maintained, unlike the sidewalks. As someone who uses a manual wheelchair due to cerebral palsy, curb cuts are very important to me. Dayton doesn't have them, so if we look at the skyline together, we'll be making an arduous trip.

I don't mind your staring at the wheelchair, but the most important detail you should know about me is that I was born on a Tuesday. According to the American poet Robert Louis Stevenson, a Tuesday's child is full of grace—perhaps contrary to appearances, in my case. *This* Tuesday's child was born in an ambulance on the way to the hospital, three months prematurely. Before you decide whether I'm worth dinner *and* cocktails at your favorite Dayton restaurant, you should know that I've always taken the circumstances of my birth as a sign that I am destined to go places, specifically by leaving Dayton.

Because of the technical innovations that Charles F. Kettering and Wilbur and Orville Wright brought to Dayton in the early twentieth century, the city became an industrial center. I've never felt any particular pride about Dayton's industrial innovations, since the Dayton workforce wasn't widely accessible to people with disabilities until the stop-to-stop paratransit system, a transportation system that is under the Regional Transit Authority (RTA), was established in the 1970s. Of course, *my* workforce isn't solely inaccessible to people with disabilities. If I look so longingly at photos of the Chicago skyline, it's partially because I'm a performer with a PhD in theater who isn't working in her chosen field. The theater industry is arguably *especially* inaccessible to people with disabilities, and Dayton's buildings illustrate why. The largest theater company has a revolving stage, a stage design that makes both blocking a wheelchair onstage and finding room for it when I'm offstage more difficult. The largest theater company that hires local performers, as opposed to hosting touring Broadway shows, doesn't have a ramp at the building's entrance. There are many dedicated local performers starting local companies that produce original work, but they don't make large enough profits to buy their rehearsal or performance spaces. They have neither the legal clearance nor the financial resources to update their buildings in order to make those buildings compliant with the standards in the Americans With Disabilities Act.

I know, you're making eyes at me over that cocktail because you want me to stop ranting about the Dayton arts scene, or the lack of one. You do have very expressive eyes, which is why I want you to know I'm not an egotistical date. You're right. The story of an artist who lacks funding could be a narrative in *any* city; we did agree you're paying for these cocktails, right? In this city, though, that same lack of resources is present in every field. The bailout for the American recession wasn't a bailout for individual cities. The Rust Belt was a nickname given to a collection of states, Ohio included, that were vital to the success of the automobile industry. Now that nickname, the Rust Belt, is an apt simile for Dayton's financial straits. We're all tightening our belts, but the buckles are so rusty from years of tightening that we can barely move them anymore. As my cousin from Buffalo, New York, put it in his text to me: "Didn't Dayton used to be famous for inventing flight or something? What is it famous for now? Opioid addictions and a shooting, right?"

When my cousin sent that text, Dayton, Ohio, was in the news daily. The newscasters were covering the August 2019 shooting in the Oregon District, where ten people were killed, including the perpetrator. I don't know anyone who was killed in the Oregon District that night. The shooting didn't change my opinions about gun control or how our current model of masculinity affects young men. [Yes, I probably should've warned you that I talk about politics every time I go on a date.] It showed me how I felt about *my city*. I despaired because I couldn't protect *my streets* or restore *my city's* reputation. I always measured my own success by whether and for how long I managed to escape Dayton, Ohio.

After all, I'm a Tuesday's child. If I'm full of grace, it's because I'm meant to grace a theater stage in a city where the theater marquees' lights are large enough to be an impressive part of a skyline. Even if I escaped Dayton, it would still be *my city*. My whole childhood fits within the breadth of that tightened Rust Belt. My first (free) theater shows played in Dayton parks. I gathered arrowheads in Dayton woods, then returned them. And yes, I looked longingly into the windows of clothing boutiques in the Oregon District. I am a Tuesday's child in a city of Tuesday's children who uncomplainingly tighten their belts without casting down their eyes. I can tell you're afraid to take my hand, because you want to know what is coming next for us. I promise I'll be here tomorrow.

Riverscape

BETSY HUGHES

Through river currents flows the potent blood
of settlers, bold events in Dayton's past,
of life and death, fertility and flood;
the memory of history will last.
Beside the river, strolling on this day,
we rest a moment near the hillside's brink
and ponder while we watch the fountains spray;
about the present here-and-now we think.
This scene provides a panoramic view
to witness while we pause by river's edge;
imbued with faith we face our prospects — New! —
to these unknowns our eager hopes we pledge.
The past becomes the future in this flux,
this riverscape, this always flowing crux.

First published online by Five Rivers MetroParks

Grills, Gyros, and a Few Greasy Spoons: A Fourty-Year Downtown Dayton Journey

JUDD PLATTENBURG

The smell of bacon and burgers on a flat iron grill, fries in the deep fryer, and somebody yelling for the waiter to bring more coffee. And you can't forget the scent of cigarettes thick throughout the diner. That was the scene in the late 1970s at Simple Simon, a short-order grill on East Third and St. Clair, where a cook named Ace, looking like he was working off a hangover, was cooking a variety of fried foods on the grill with everybody at the counter sitting and watching.

I was from the suburbs but started working downtown in 1977. I was a high school intern, who, after studying printing technologies, got a job at a dingy little print shop where all the machines were held together with rubber bands and whatever else they could find. An older lady named Camelia Crawford, whose husband was a printer but had died some years back, now owned the place. It was run in an old-school manner, down to the point that our parking plan consisted of a roll of dimes we would each get once a week so that we could run out at lunch and refill the four-hour parking meters.

I've worked downtown ever since then, not far from that original print shop, and I've seen Dayton go through evolution and change, with more than one mini-revival over the years. What I'm seeing in 2020 feels different, making me reminisce about my downtown Dayton journey that began more than 40 years ago.

The print shop, named J. Frank Reist Service, was on Third Street in what's now the Fire Blocks district. Back then, it was a bit sketchy, but it's being fixed up and is on its way to becoming another addition to Dayton's new downtown scene. There was a dirty bookstore next door that always smelled like cherry perfume and the guy who ran it was kind of short. I'm pretty sure he always had a pistol tucked in the back of his pants. The Century Bar was still around the corner but back in the day, before it morphed into the fancy bourbon bar it is today, it was just a cool older bar that served these big greasy burgers that were great.

Wympee was up the street at the corner of Wayne and Third and existed in the same realm as the other short-order joints with the smell of grease and cigarettes. The building is still there with the name embellished on the side—you can't miss it—but it's either been empty since its closing or has served as the location for experimental restaurants. The short-order diners were big back then, with a cook preparing easy food and customers sitting at a counter watching—a common scene in the guts of so many American cities. The other old short order in Dayton still standing is White Tower. They had what they called The Famous Butter Burger, and most people I knew thought it went fine with a hangover. Its two original locations now exist under different names.

A fixture back then was a guy everybody called Rags. He was almost a legend to many of us in 1970s downtown Dayton. Nobody at the time knew his real name was Elias Joseph Barauskas, and that he was an Army corporal who served in World War II. He wore the same set of clothing for years until they were nothing but rags tied to his body and feet. He wore them through the cold winter and never complained until he collapsed in front of Simple Simon on May 5, 1980, and died the same day at Miami Valley hospital. Rags used to hang out at the library and read a lot, and spent time in the alley behind the print shop where I worked. The few times I spoke to him, he didn't have much to say, other than that nobody needed to know about him. There is very little written about him, but the small brushes in life I had with him were experiences I will never forget.

Friday was always payday. The Winters Bank Tower, soon to be renamed the Kettering Tower, was still new, just completed in 1970. It was always a marvel to me and somewhat intimidating to go into that new, glass tower and ride the large, impressive escalator up to the second floor bank lobby and cash my check.

With cash in hand, I took a short walk across the street to the food court in the lower Arcade Square, which had just gone through its first major renovation and reopened in 1980. The Arcade was a happening place in the early '80s when it reopened. They had taken out the main floor to open a downstairs food court full of small eateries, but it was always hard to find a place to sit. I think at one point, they even hired a guard to help move people out when they were done eating, which I thought defeated the whole purpose of trying to get people down there. My best memory was a place that sold gyros, a place with Greek name that started with a Z, but I can't remember much more. The guy who made my gyro played guitar in a local band called The Slugs, who always sold out when they played the Walnut Hills (when it was on First Street). I felt special having my gyro handmade by a local celebrity.

Courthouse Square had also undergone a major renovation. There was an older, bigger courthouse where the square is located now that opened in 1884, but it was demolished in the 1970s to develop the current square. After eating at the Arcade, you could wander through an "Affair on the Square," someone's idea of a Friday lunchtime party atmosphere. I think the food vendors then were the predecessors to today's food trucks. I always felt a little out of place at these events, as they promoted them for "professionals" in the office buildings, and I never quite fit in. Instead, I'd go over to Rike's, which was just across Second Street where the Schuster Center is now, and wander through for bargains before I had to rush back to work.

The revival that downtown Dayton is undergoing is very exciting. I love it and am involved in a lot of ways. But I think a lot of that love and excitement comes from the experience of being there decades earlier, seeing businesses come and go. I've watched different initiatives to revive Dayton that usually start strong and then appear to slow down a bit; we deemed them a failure only to now recognize that they took hold more than we thought. The Dayton Dragons, RiverScape and the whole riverway, the Schuster Performing Arts Center, the Oregon District, even losing most of that majestic newspaper building on Ludlow Street (Remember the Embassy?)—all have helped shape Dayton in the twenty-first century.

This city has a rhythm, slow and steady with change, but always moving forward. Being able to witness a lot of these little things that aren't there anymore, but are still recorded in our memories, is what makes it real. I can't wait to see where it takes us next.

The Canal Street Tavern 2013

MATTHEW SZOZDA

Here, at the corner of First and North Patterson,
We swaddle ourselves in the sounds of this liquid devotional.
We find our forgiveness behind barstool pews and stained glass windows,
Wooden floors with songs buried inside of their grain.
Our local confessional.

In the shadows of the pulpit,
She moves like a flamingo.
Shaking water from her feet,
Body Straight,
Legs bent,
Toes curling like well-dressed perms.
A mysterious type of wild.

A foreign deity creeps its way into my skin.
Not the punk rock scene I was confirmed into.
Not *Jasper the Colossal* or *The Nightbeast*,
Just pure Kentucky twang.
Ma Crow preaching a banjo like a hurricane of birds.
My clumsy drunk just trying to keep up.
Born again,
In electric sanctity.
In this construction paper church.
A fresh baptism for a flooded city.
All are welcome.

She accepts my offering.
A communion,
Tastes like peppermint schnapps and cigarettes,
And for a moment,
I believed.

A Special Memory, Even Amid the What-Ifs

ONEITA JACKSON

Our eight-month relationship began with a bag of Mikesell's potato chips.

Bob McGruder and I both grew up in Dayton, so every time I went home, I grabbed a bag of the hometown favorites for him. The potato-chip exchanges were quiet, mutual. When I saw Bob coming toward my desk, which is across from his office, I'd place the Mikesell's on the file cabinet in front of me, then flick them toward him with my thumb and index finger.

Towering over my desk, he'd give me a warm "This girl is crazy" smile. He'd say, "Thank you," I'd give the chin-up nod, and he'd slide by in his deliberate manner. It was a fourteen-second ritual I relished.

And it was part of my plan.

The idea was for me, a lowly one-year intern, to get to know Bob, the top dog, through the subtle moments. Bob hadn't been in the office the day I was interviewed. I knew he had an open-door policy, so I figured I'd waltz through the clear glass doors to his office after our relationship had grown.

Now, I wish I'd kicked the doors in. I should have told him we had more in common than our Gem City roots. Bob's indefatigable spirit reminded me of my daddy, who also died of cancer in 1990.

Seeing Bob walk around the newsroom brought back memories of my father's tenacity as he played tug-of-war with colon cancer. I wish I'd told my homeboy how I admired his poise, his dignity.

I thought I had time.

I know it's selfish, but I'm feeling cheated because I don't have a litany of Bob McGruder anecdotes to tell—no "I never would've gotten that job if Bob hadn't called up so-and-so" accounts, no "If it hadn't been for Bob" appreciation stories. But I am glad that just for a moment, God allowed me to be in the presence of one of the unequivocal avatars of journalism.

Before I got to the *Detroit Free Press*, I'd heard about the No. 1 man at the paper. I was starstruck when I met him. I've had significant encounters with celebrities and remained unimpressed. But meeting Bob was an honor.

I was even more honored one day in February, when Bob walked over to my desk, smiled and handed me a ten-pack of snack-size bags of plain Mikesell's. I was overcome! My potato-chip plan was beginning to bear spuds.

I was just getting up the moxie to take the walk through the glass doors to Bob's office when I found out that he was away getting new cancer treatments. Then, I became anxious. The what-ifs gnawed at me. Fear set in. I felt like I was reliving my daddy's struggle with cancer. I thought Bob was getting better, not worse.

Just before Bob passed, *Free Press* employees signed a giant sixtieth birthday card. My message read: "I got ten bags of Mikesell's; when you comin' to get 'em, man?" Quietly, I feared he wouldn't be back.

Two weeks ago, we got an email saying that Bob had been taken to a hospice. I knew it was coming, but I wasn't ready. I called my mommy, who knew Bob only from my mad dashes to the gas station to get his chips and through my Bob McGruder conversations. She said, "All we can do now is pray."

Before my daddy died, she had said you have to turn it over to Jesus. And that's what I did in Bob's case. "Lord, please make him better, if it's your will," I prayed.

The Lord's will is done, and though I never got to tell Bob thank you for giving me a job after my internship, somehow I know he knows I'm grateful.

I'll be going home in a few weeks. And I won't leave Dayton without our Mikesell's potato chips. As I drive up I-75, I'll munch on a bag in Bob's memory.

Originally published in the Detroit Free Press, *April 18, 2002.*

Mr. (Willis [Bing]) Davis Has Class

LEAH DEALOIA

Art's necessity and Art's joy
Meet at the node of the Artist's
      Honesty:
             Something I discovered
      While learning to make art through
Mr. Davis' Class.

          But.
Tempted, I occasionally followed
      Kiki in her clogs and
      Bob with the black swatch in his blond hair
Up the stairs to the little room,
      Where talk turned to
      Pot and pills.

          But.
My mind was fingering a broken Cray-Pas
      In Prussian Blue, oil and wax, or palest
           Watercolors never tamed by will alone.
In that secret upper room, I'd make
      My excuses, trip back
          Down
              the
                  stairs.

          And.
Return to our class project: the problem of
      Transmogrifying an ancient lace-up ankle boot
          Into a futuristic objet d'art.
As now I wrestle with these words,
      Transmogrifying them, as best I can, into

The ineffable.
That was the lesson.
What I was taught.
What I practice.

Because.
Mr. Davis had, and has, and always will have
Class.

A City Worth Fighting For

SHELLEY KURTZ SOMMER

There are two pictures on my desk in my home twenty miles south of Boston, one of the old Carnegie Library in Xenia and the other of my family during a recent visit to Carillon Park. Even now, nearly forty years after moving away, these pictures are daily reminders of my deep connection to the Dayton area.

I lived in Xenia as a child until 1974, when my family lost our house in the tornado and moved to Dayton. I spent my teenage years in Oakwood and then went to the University of Dayton, where I cheered on the Flyers, ate Milano's subs, and lived in the neighborhood then called "the ghetto." My family still lives in Ohio. In fact, my sister now teaches at UD, and while I am now a school librarian at a private school in Massachusetts, the picture of the Xenia Library continues to inspire my work. It is the place where I stacked as many books as I could carry home and began imagining what it would be like to live in a big city.

In Dayton, I was active in local Democratic politics, working primarily on campaigns for the former mayor, Paul Leonard. It was through his campaigns that I came to know Dayton's neighborhoods and gain a stronger sense of the city's history and potential. Now, during my annual trips back to Dayton, I see the changes that I follow on Instagram and the *Dayton Daily News* app. I see the revitalization taking place downtown, and most notably, the dedication of people like Mayor Nan Whaley who are working to make Dayton the wonderful hometown I remember. I'm watching the renewal of the Dayton Arcade, the restoration of the Grand Staircase at the Dayton Art Institute, and the bold steps UD is taking to invest in Dayton's future.

This past August, as I watched reports about the tragic mass shooting in the Oregon District, I felt simultaneously horrified and proud. The horrified reaction is easy to understand, but I was also proud of the community spirit that was so evident to anyone watching news reports from Dayton.

I am not viewing Dayton through rose-colored glasses. The challenges faced by mid-sized American cities, especially the impact of the opioid crisis and the economic challenges caused by the decline in the number of manufacturing jobs, are certainly real. But I know Dayton's history of innovation—and am reminded of it when I look at my picture of Carillon Park.

I often tell friends in Boston that Dayton was the original Silicon Valley. Like San Francisco today, Dayton was once home to people tinkering in garages—or bicycle shops—and creating the future. My students know all about Dayton's rich history, and often see displays of books about the Wright Brothers and Paul Laurence Dunbar in their Massachusetts school library.

I have faith in the spirit of innovation that is woven into Dayton's history. Dayton is a city worth fighting for.

Why We Left Columbus

MICHAEL MCGOVERN

At the end of October 2019, my wife and I moved sixty miles west down I-70 from Columbus to Dayton, where we grew up. We received a lot of confused looks when we told people—as if leaving a thriving capital city for a struggling Rust Belt community a fifth its size isn't a perfectly reasonable choice to make.

It's nothing against Columbus. Over our four years there, we both hit our stride professionally. We each picked up master's degrees from Ohio State—though neither of us acquired any interest in the Buckeyes. And most importantly, we built a strong network of close friends, particularly in our little corner of Franklinton, a neighborhood just west of downtown.

Columbus is a lovely, growing city that is thriving economically and culturally. Which is exactly why we felt compelled to move home to Dayton.

Like much of the country, people and resources are being concentrated in fewer places in Ohio. While Columbus has seen strong economic growth and investment, much of the rest of the state—particularly older industrial cities like Dayton—continue to struggle. If you were to pull Columbus out of Ohio, our state's economic outlook would look much more bleak.

Data indicates that much of Columbus's growth has come at the expense of other communities in Ohio. This was certainly my experience—many of the folks I met there moved from smaller cities for school or work. Which is a perfectly reasonable thing to do—it's exactly why my wife and I came there. But there are repercussions for these other places, as talent and resources are sucked away.

For progressives, this pattern should be especially concerning politically. While Columbus becomes more Democratic, other places in the state become less so. Republicans have rigged with maps extreme gerrymandering, but we aren't doing ourselves any favors when we all move to the same couple cities. Democrats can't hope to retake the statehouse or congressional seats if we live in fewer and fewer places.

Dayton has experienced all of these challenges. But like so many other small and mid-sized Rust Belt cities, it has seen a remarkable resurgence. Population is inching up for the first time in decades. New development is coming to downtown and millennials are fixing up homes in historic neighborhoods. Unlike the gentrification seen in Columbus, the high rates of vacancy that Dayton is still struggling with means that no one is getting displaced. The city is not without its problems, and development has yet to fully benefit historically marginalized communities, particularly African Americans. But Dayton has turned a corner.

None of this is unique to Dayton. Small and mid-sized cities across Ohio—and across the Midwest—are being revitalized and recreated by young people who know that not everyone has to live in New York or San Francisco—or even Columbus. The cultural amenities that once set these cities apart have made their way to smaller cities. Places like Akron, Warren, and even Chillicothe are becoming vibrant again because folks are choosing to commit to them. You can still find a hip coffee shop in Youngstown and a good brewery in Mansfield—but there is also the charm of a city with a deep history that can once again be something special.

The past still looms large in cities like Dayton, but the city is redefining itself into something new. Rather than recreate an idealized version of the past that left behind many of its residents, it is becoming something better: a community that is more equitable and more inclusive; that is putting a new spin on its history of innovation and invention.

I'm not saying everyone should move from Columbus to Dayton (even though they should). But I hope that more young people from cities around the state and the region that are reinventing themselves will consider moving home to be a part of something exciting. Not as some sort of big city savior, but as someone working to build a community that is better than what was there before.

The thing is, Columbus and cities like it will be successful regardless of whether transplants like me are there. But if you're from a city that is still trying to make its turnaround, your presence may really make a difference. Authenticity has become a millennial trope, but it's truly what these cities have to offer.

I loved my life in Columbus, but I'm excited to jump head first into a new community that has incredible potential. There's opportunity like this all around Ohio and the Midwest, you just have to be willing to give it a chance.

A version of this piece originally appeared in the Columbus Dispatch.

Loving Living in Dayton

BOB TAFT

Time flies when life is good. It's hard to believe that my wife, Hope and I have lived in the Dayton area for more than a dozen years.

The people of Dayton have been very welcoming. We've made many friends and found it easy as new residents of Dayton to become engaged in the life of the community.

The older I get, the more I love history, and Dayton is a town that proudly displays its past. Serving on the board of Dayton History at Carillon Park introduced me to the remarkable inventors and entrepreneurs who built the city, to the devastating Dayton Flood of 1913 that led to the creation of a pioneering dam and levee system, and to the amazing Wright Brothers who made Ohio the birthplace of aviation. The strong community support of new displays and exhibits at Dayton History the past few years has been inspiring to behold.

Dayton provides multiple opportunities for schoolchildren to experience how our history has shaped the present—from Carillon Park to the National Air Force Museum, the many Wright brothers sites and SunWatch Indian Village. We can be confident that the children of Dayton will grow up with a strong sense of their history.

We are happy that Dayton is a patriotic community. As the home of Wright-Patterson Air Force Base and the Dayton VA Medical Center, Daytonians have a love of country and appreciate the sacrifices made by those who have served and continue to serve to keep us safe. My favorite event each year is the Memorial Day concert at Carillon Park where Army, Navy, Marine Corps, Air Force and Coast Guard veterans rise to be recognized as the Dayton Philharmonic Orchestra plays the music from their service theme songs.

We have enjoyed Dayton's many educational and arts opportunities, and I would highlight two in which I have been fortunate to become involved: the Dayton Literary Peace Prize (DLLP) and Air Camp, both homegrown in the last ten-fifteen years through the initiative of visionary local leaders. The DLLP, building on the Dayton Peace Accords, recognizes and attracts to Dayton each year world-class authors of fiction and non-fiction, bringing international attention to our city. Air Camp attracts hundreds of students from across the country each summer to be inspired by STEM learning experiences based on aviation and aeronautics. Science teachers benefit from project-based learning courses offered by Air Camp.

Hope and I have taken advantage of the unique recreational and outdoor opportunities available in the Dayton area. We live near the Little Miami, a national and state scenic river, and have spent many a day paddling on its well-shaded waters. Hope helped to form Little Miami River Kleeners and Watershed Network to protect and preserve the river for future generations. She has received strong community support for this initiative.

I am an avid cyclist, and there could be no better place in the country for cycling. The Dayton area has hundreds of miles of paved bike trails. We live near Xenia, a trail hub, and I most frequently ride the Little Miami Scenic Trail which is part of the Ohio River to Lake Erie Trail that is nearing completion and will connect Cincinnati to Cleveland. The Friends of the Little Miami State Park, a local citizens group which I have supported, helps repair and maintain some fifty miles of the trail.

Hope and I have lived for a number of years in Cincinnati and Columbus, but Dayton has been the best possible home for us these past 12 years. We would like to thank everyone who works and volunteers to make our adopted city such an exceptional place to live.

The Ellis Island of Dayton: An Interview with Islom Shakhbandarov

SHANNON SHELTON MILLER

For much of his life, Islom Shakhbandarov had no place he could call home.

His Ahiska Turkish community was stateless for much of the twentieth century, experiencing deportation from the former Soviet republic of Georgia during World War II by Josef Stalin, and ethnic cleansing and oppression in the 1980s and 1990s in Russia and other former Soviet republics where they'd been dispersed.

Shakhbandarov arrived in Abilene, Texas, in 2004, not long after the United States granted refugee status to 15,000 Ahiska Turks. About four months later, he moved to Boise, Idaho, to live with a grandfather and uncles who had already made the journey to the U.S. Shortly after getting married in Boise, he and his wife moved to Dayton, a place they could finally consider home.

"The north part of Dayton has historically been full of immigrants from different backgrounds," he said. "They told me it was like the Ellis Island of Dayton. All the Eastern European immigrants came here and that's where all the Turkish immigrants came when we arrived in the United States."

He and his wife moved with about six other Ahiska Turkish families in 2007. In 2009, close to 100 families had settled in Old North Dayton. By 2011, more than 200 families called the area home.

"When I came here in 2007, I found that Dayton was a very nice city," he said. "What struck me most was the housing affordability. In Boise, Idaho, I remembered the cheapest home you could get close to was $150,000-$160,000. For refugees who just came to the United States, working for $7 an hour in labor jobs, it was an unreachable dream for us to own any property in such high volumes."

Their settlement in Dayton wasn't just coincidence. During the last two decades, Dayton has worked to establish itself as a destination for newcomers from other countries, touting immigrant-friendly policies, affordable housing and job opportunities to help curb population declines and bring new energy to the city. In 2011, the City of Dayton commission adopted the Welcome Dayton plan, a community initiative to actively promote immigrant integration. Leaders of the Ahiska Turkish community provided consultation to city leaders in the development of the Welcome Dayton plan, sharing ways the city could help immigrants adjust to their new lives in the city.

Shakhbandarov is proud of the way the Ahiska Turks help revitalize Old North Dayton, filling empty homes and beautifying their neighborhoods. He praised Dayton's affordability, schools and access to safe housing for newcomers like himself. He felt the established Old North Dayton community—initially reluctant about the presence of the Ahiska Turks—grew to embrace them when they saw their positive impact on the community.

"People start seeing the changes we bring, that we bring revitalization," he said. "We invested in the neighborhood that nobody wanted to invest in and that people were running away from. In our community, especially the old folks and some of the political elite, they started appreciating that and they started supporting us."

In 2012, he founded the Ahiska Turkish American Community Center as a gathering place to help facilitate connections between community members and integrate new arrivals to the Dayton community.

Firmly settled into life in Dayton with his wife and two sons, Shakhbandarov continues to serve as a cheerleader for the city.

"You can live a pretty decent life here," he said. "I think the future of Dayton depends on the future of America in general. There's always room for improvement, but for past ten years, the city has overcome a lot after losing GM and all those big manufacturers. Life is coming back to downtown and they're announcing new investment in West Dayton. I'm really hoping things will keep changing for the better, but it will also help if the national government finds out which direction they will go."

2019

What Angry Winds Can Do

JOHN GORMAN

There were woods here once,
On this hillside we passed each day
On our way to school.
Across the street, too,
Those trees hiding big buildings
We knew were there but
Couldn't see from the road.
What buildings we could see
Weren't much to look at:
Gas stations and pizza places,
Drive-thru liquor stores attached to
Bars we were warned never to enter.
Apartments, too, ones best avoided
If you could, though not everybody could,
Not everybody can, when it comes to
Places like that. We'd drive by and
Marvel at the trees and their leaves, and
Shake our heads at those buildings,
At where people live and go and
Let themselves be found.
The mid-town foliage surrounded and
Obscured so much we disregarded
With a look and a thought,
"How pretty this all looks in the
Blinding summer sun/in the
Lightly falling rain/in the snow/
At dawn/in the late-evening dusk,
And what a wonderful city Dayton
Is to be from," all the while knowing
We weren't wrong.

Those trees are gone now,
From both sides of the road,

Torn apart and uprooted by angry winds.
Same goes for those buildings,
The ones where people lived and drank,
Where they got pizza and gas.
As for those we never saw,
Buried deep in the woods?
Their advanced press lied,
They weren't anything special.
There was a lid on the world,
A mask covered its face, and
It was easy to let that mask
Convince you that it didn't matter
What was underneath.
The mask sufficed, the look plenty,
The trees enough, their magic and love.
Without them there the bones are showing.
That lid came off, the magic got out,
The love evaporated, and the wind left
Wreckage in their place, in ways that feel
Unending, if not everlasting.
Now when people pass by each day
On their way to school or work or
Some place else, they see what remains
Of what was here and think to themselves,
"So that's all this was all along, and
Here so little of it's left." They can't help
What this does to their faces, nor
What it's done to the air.

Invisible Ink

CYNTHIA R. KEEFER

Memorial Day evening 2019 bawling winds coiled tree trunks the way red stripes corkscrew up white candy canes. Limbs do-si-do with partners. Fifteen tornadoes divided before the bell struck midnight. Each took a path. Bird nests split. Hollow raccoon homes opened. Squirrel litters fell out on the ground and the wind tunnels dumped thick hidden tree honeycombs on the ground. Houses were imploded and exploded, roofs torn off in no ways alike. Porches flew away and porches next door stayed. Garages fell on cars and protected cars. Trees crushed driveway-parked cars flatter than junkyard crushers. County townships were being drawn up in new lines charted on maps "Hit" and "Unhit."

Loud tornado sirens wailed for me to take cover. Me and my pillow entered my walk-in closet. Then I sat on the floor and wondered, "What was I thinking? For a long winter's nap?" The battery-driven radio auctioned off street names bearing the E4 torment taking place across Harrison Township, just part of its twenty-mile path. I knew those streets. I lived a childhood on those streets. I realized Dayton Children's hospital was directly in the path of destruction.

Had I heard God declare "Enough?" The devil winds divided around the sick babies, toddlers, young people, and spared the caretakers as well? The tornado did not bring down a light pole, a flag pole, or an awning. It harmed no waiting, needed ambulances nor hospital generator.

As a septuagenarian, I remember more than seventy-five years ago my childhood home. We lived across the street from my Uncle Bob and my Great Aunt Nell, my paternal grandmother's sister. North of them, past one house, lived Dad's sister, Grace, her husband, and their two sons. Three houses beyond, my Dad's brother, wife, and three sons resided. The street was lined with roosting Resslers. My paternal grandparents, Pop and Mom Ressler, lived around the corner. And next door to my grandparents lived their eldest child Aunt Ethel, her husband, and four children. As a child, I assumed all neighborhoods were made up of cousins. That was the way it was for me. We were all strung out along Lindale and I was anchored at both ends. My maternal grandparents lived at Neva at the other end of Lindale, before it was cut through. Today, I live in a newer neighborhood and am lucky to have cousins a few sidewalk steps from me.

Our old childhood neighborhood was struck by tornadoes Memorial Day evening. Daylight revealed destruction. The barber shop with fifty years of hair clippings was destroyed by shrapnel. The shell fragments left one head-washing basin that clung from the only standing wall. A lone vacant barber chair waited under a wide blue sky. "Next?" I could hear Barber Jim's calm voice in my mind. Jim had a way with young children. They never cried at the buzz of the shears in Jim's hands.

"It sounds like an oncoming train" is the infamous description of tornado survivors. Cousin Patty headed for her basement when her home imploded. Her friend threw her under the dining table then laid on top of her until the night grew quiet. They were unhurt.

Years ago, Uncle Fred opened a full-service filling station at Dixie and Neff Roads. He lived behind the station with his wife, Mary Lou, and their daughter Rae Lou. Aunt Mary Lou made the best fudge in Harrison Township! And probably the county. She sold her fudge in her husband's filling station, pre-Board of Health days. We cousins hung around on peanut butter fudge-making day, Wednesday. It was our favorite. Aunt Mary Lou generously provided us with what she called "tastes." Those squares of heaven filled the palms of our young hands. The tornado decimated Fred's place, leaving a grass lot with not one stick, stone, nor step. I feel badly for the present-day owners, but I am glad Fred's family did not live to see the destruction of all they had worked so very hard to establish.

Across from Uncle Fred's stands a four-room schoolhouse, Northridge B. My mother, her sister and brother started their climb up the education ladder in that school, followed by my cousins. Spinster teachers earned a wage at that school in a time and place where married women were barred from earning a wage during the hard times of wars and depression. Men were off to war after their training in Triangle Park. Men had hopped trains for promised jobs in Detroit, a lie often told. Dr. Duckwall lived on the peninsula formed by Siebenthaler and Fieldstone and Dixie. The doctor had doctored in the Civil War. In retirement his unmarried daughter took care of the centurion. A teacher's salary would have helped them out. The Duckwalls rented out their garage to one of my uncles for a source of income when pensions were scarce and Medicare not a choice.

When my father was young, he and his brother were given the task by their father, Pop Ressler, to gather river rocks from the shallow Stillwater River. Earl and Ralph pushed and pulled river rocks in wagons and wheelbarrows way across Lincoln Park (DeWeese Parkway today). The stones rode up Siebenthaler Hill and down the other side to their father's waiting trowel.

The day after the tornadoes, I stood in the golden sunlight that danced off Pop Ressler's river-rock chimney. Standing like a rocket, ready to launch at my grandfather's home nestled in Siebenthaler's Curve, it filled me with pride. Sam Ressler built something that fifteen tornadoes could not knock down.

Samuel William Ressler, stonemason, 1878-1962, born of German immigrants on farmland east of the Great Miami River and west of Troy Pike along Needmore Road. The farm was just at the end of the covered bridge. Needmore curved around the farm then. It did not go straight up the hill to Troy Pike. Great Aunt Nell told me of friendly Indians canoeing by the farm as she and her mother Barbara Ressler hung their laundry on grape vines.

Sam, a six-foot, quiet stonemason, erected pillars, custom masonry stonescapes at the entryways of intersecting Ridge Avenue streets. They dot the entryways and driveways and form walls the length of Ridge Avenue. Fieldstone and Ridge remain a handiwork.

Pop Ressler took care of his neighborhood, walking the installation ditches in the early 1950s when the city of Dayton incorporated us. Pop lit and hung lanterns from wooden sawhorses along the middle of the streets' city-dug water line ditches. The lanterns were to divert cars from driving into ditches. We had no street lights in the country.

I say that the city incorporated us, but it was three-fourths of us. At the first meeting, in my parent's basement, the city talked of an invisible corporation line across Fifth Ave. (Today called Woodhaven, the city erased our Fifth Ave. stating they already had one.) When the day came, three weeks after school started, a city truck came and pounded a visible white-painted post in the ground beside Scrafield's driveway and called it CORPORATION. It was then we saw the bottom quarter of Fifth Ave. was left in the county. The invisible demarcation line, they talked about at the basement meeting, yanked three-fourths of the neighborhood children from the Northridge county school system and assigned them desks in the city schools.

Traumatic? Ask those incoming fall seniors who still talk, a half-century plus of being forced to attend a school in which they did not own a letter sweater and attended less than a year. It seems the city did not have "something in place," so we were told, causing us not to start school until three weeks after it began for the walkers. We were the "bus kids." It was a term used in a demeaning way. One was when the principal called on the loud speaker for teachers to dismiss "the bus kids." Another was that "bus kids" ate in the gymnasium because in our hour and a half allotted time, the walkers went home for lunch! What we found out years later was that if a parent paid tuition and provided transportation their child could continue in the county school. We wondered if this applied to the principal of Northridge (soon to become superintendent), who now resided on the city side of the corporation line, or did he get a dispensation to keep his children in his county district without tuition?

Incorporation meant a policeman knocked on our door and told my father, "Your dog cannot sleep in the street! You are under city laws now and your dog must be kept in your yard when not on a leash." Dad asked nicely for the officer to explain the regulation to our ten-year-old Lassie. I didn't hear the answer. Mom ushered me off to my bedroom.

Incorporation meant our address changed, though we had not moved off the street.

Incorporation meant Dad had to remove our rabbit hutch. We were in the city now. It removed more meat from what our ration stamps allowed. And added more "meatless days" the government asked Americans to observe. One day as we stood at the butcher's case, my brother promised Mother that when he grew up he would buy her all the ration stamps she needed.

Incorporation line, visible or invisible, divided the closeness of attending a best friend and family member's Friday night football games. We sat in bleachers usually by street residents, close neighbors to neighbors.

Incorporation confined friendships into two weekend days. Make that one and a half days if you needed to do a homework project or if you had extra Saturday chores. Some of us girls ironed our father's white, starched shirts for the following week.

"Let's reminisce."

Mom Ressler directed her children and grandchildren's visit. If she asked us to sit on the front porch swing, we let the oldest, long-legged cousin "pump" us. If she invited us to sit on her couch when our young legs did not touch the carpet, we sat delicately and gingerly so as not to raise wrath with what Grandmother called "dried flood mud."

Cousin Bubba (who hated his name, Marvin) flopped on the couch cushions causing floor mud to fly out in the room and layer dust on the furniture, carpet, mantel. That is why Mom Ressler's phonograph machine was covered with a blanket.

"Did I tell you Mom and Pop Ressler met while ice skating at Lock 15 on the Miami Erie Canal?"

"Did I tell you that one hundred and six years ago, Sam Ressler rowed his two-man fishing boat to second-floor windows in Harrison Township where narrow ironing boards were laid between two neighbors' homes and people crawled across ironing boards, rescued in Pop Ressler's awaiting boat, as the thirty-five-year-old man rowed against the fierce currents that develop between two large ships or two large houses? Did I tell you of the dead horses floating by? The floating overturned wooden boxes that if turned upright were wagons of family members trying to outrun the water? That was in the 1913 flood!"

"Did I tell you about the time one of the Wright boys aviated off McCook Field, next to the Stillwater and Great Miami River's meeting point, south of the Ridge Avenue Bridge? The lad flew across two side-by-side bridges. One for car traffic, Keowee Street Bridge. And one for the bridged rails for the Interurban, a bridge of tracks. Over the Dixie Highway the plane's engine stopped. The young lad landed the plane between my maternal grandparent's house, the Lackeys and their neighbors, the McGruders' house.

It was not a landing on ground. The wing tips landed on the two neighbors' roofs, leaving the fuselage dangling like a fat grasshopper. Again an ironing board was brought to the second floor, shoved out the window, and as mother said, "the pilot shimmied and jiggered down, unhurt."

Today as I left the "Hit" neighborhood, I stopped at Northridge B. I pointed my finger at the paste-lathered papers plastered on its walls and windows. Large black block letters read CONDEMNED.

With a great shout, I laid my voice at the door.

"You cannot post a sentence on our memories! Our memories live in our dialog with our children and our children's children. We will indulge our recollections. We will keep our memories alive."

Red is the color of August

ASHLEY BETHARD

I.
Red is the color of August.
Each beautiful sunset seems
like a protest:
clouds twisted into a gaping maw
an open-faced silent scream
others breaking into some type of
Rorschach test
with no right answer.

The half-moon's edge is
sharp as a razor.
Everyone's asleep now
and we're in the same dream.

II.
I walk the yard of my childhood home
greet the trees
like old friends.
I visit the mound of dirt
where the pines once stood
rest my hand on the stump of maple
worn smooth.

I eat concord grapes off the vine
like I did when I was a child.
My father tosses one into his mouth
tells me the grapevines have been here
for 70 years.

He's been cleaning up the place,
I can tell.
The backyard fence is gone
and metal stakes removed.

There are no remnants of the pool left,
no more swingset poles
littering the ground.
He is preparing
getting rid of
putting away a
way of life.

He talks about the lilacs again
for the second summer in a row.
They still block the road.
He ponders his choices:
cut them back, transplant them,
or remove them altogether.
Oh hell, he says. *I'm not staying here anyway.*
I don't ask
but I assume it means he will sell.

Later I realize it could mean something else:
the way all of us
don't stay
the way all of us
become gone.

I take it as a lesson
don't waste energy on things that don't matter.
I take it as a reminder
of the ways we trick ourselves into
thinking there will be
a tomorrow and not a gone.

I hold it close.
I guard my heart against self-sabotage.

III.
It feels strange to be on vacation
when the world is falling apart.
The world has always been falling apart,
it's true

but now we're in a cash-only town
tucked away in the mountains.

When the man working the parking booth
greeted us with "Ohio! Where at?"
his half-toothed smile dropped
when we said, *Dayton*.
"Oh, you had some trouble out there,"
he said, shaking his head.

I thought
trouble used to mean the weather —
like lightning at the beach
or rain at a picnic.

I thought yes,
if trouble meant
blood from 9 lives gone
staining the sidewalk where I live.
How unfair it is that I can be so precious with language
in a world so reckless with lives.

When I get home
I cut 9 flowers from my garden.
I leave them at the altar.

In memory of those lost in the shooting in Dayton, Ohio, on August 4, 2019:
Jordan Cofer, Lois Oglesby, Derrick Fudge, Thomas McNichols, Beatrice
Warren-Curtis, Nicholas Cumer, Monica Brickhouse, Logan Turner, and
Saeed Saleh.

"I Just Witnessed a Mass Shooting"

An Interview with Anthony Reynolds

SHANNON SHELTON MILLER

Like hundreds of other Daytonians in the early hours of August 4, Anthony Reynolds, then thirty-one, was enjoying a night out in the Oregon District. At 1:05 a.m., he'd just left a bar with his cousin and estimates he was no more than ten or fifteen feet from the back of a line of people waiting to enter a different bar when he heard the first shots.

"I wasn't aware it was a gunshot at first," Reynolds said.

But after the second shot, the third shot, and so many more after that, he knew there was trouble. His first thoughts were of a fight gone wrong, perhaps a shootout between rivals.

"I still didn't think it was a mass shooting until I heard the rapid fire," he said. "I was just yelling to everyone—run. It's a mass shooting, it's a mass shooting!"

I fell asleep around 11:30 p.m. Saturday, August 3. The last news brief I read before I shut off my phone focused on the mass murder in El Paso, Texas, where a gunman entered a Walmart with the intent of killing people of Hispanic descent, and gunned down twenty-two people.

As I powered up my phone the next morning around 8 a.m., I saw push notifications alerting me that nine people had been killed. I thought more casualties had been counted in El Paso.

No, this was Dayton. In the eight hours I had been sleeping, this uniquely American-style tragedy had come to my town.

I read the official news accounts, then turned to social media to get the raw, unfiltered stories from people who might have been there. That's how I stumbled onto Reynolds' Facebook page and his message stamped around 1:30 a.m.

"O my god bruh i just witnessed a mass shooting in the Oregon District so many dead!"

Reporters nationwide had already found Reynolds and began to reach out to him for comment. I messaged him with my phone number, and he called me as well. By the time we talked around noon, he had repeated the story dozens of times, but thankfully was willing to do it once more.

Reynolds had the opportunity to get a look at the shooter, whose name we'd later learn through press conferences and news reports. "I saw it was a white man dressed in black with an AK-style gun and his face covered, then I saw bodies falling all around me. I just went into survival mode. It was fear. Once the bodies started dropping and the crowd started running, I just wanted to get home to my family, my daughters (twelve and ten), my fiancée. You think you want to stop and help and be a hero, but it's just fear. I was scared the next bullet would hit me."

The thought of being killed before his wedding date—July 19, 2020—to his high school sweetheart and longtime partner, also devastated him, he said.

That's why he kept running.

In addition to the initial post, Reynolds also posted a live video to Facebook, prompting calls from journalists from around the world. After leaving the Oregon District, he got in his car, drove home and stayed in the car to field calls from reporters until 6 a.m.

"It probably wasn't the most healthy way to handle it, but it was all I could do," he said. "When I got home, I kissed my fiancée and our two daughters."

And he still had to report to work at GE Aviation later that morning.

"I pulled up to the job shaking, but my boss told me to just go home. He said, 'We got this here.'"

As Reynolds continued to tell his story, he wanted to shift gears a bit to talk about Dayton and the resilience of Dayton residents. He proudly described himself as a "born and raised Daytonian," who grew up in West Dayton. He went to Dunbar High School, was a graduate of Clark State Community College, and was pursuing a bachelor's degree at Franklin University.

While he didn't know any of the nine Oregon District shooting victims personally, he said he knew people with family members who had been killed. That unfortunately wasn't surprising—Dayton can feel like a close-knit community at times.

"We all grew up on the west side and we all know each other," he said.

Reynolds also wanted reporters to focus on those who had lost their lives, and what could be done to prevent this from happening again.

"I just want people to focus on the victims," Reynolds said. "Let's not turn this into another 'dialogue.' We had two shootings in one day. Let's start making things happen."

His comments were prescient. At a vigil that Sunday evening, members of a crowd gathered to mourn the victims began shouting "do something" at Ohio Gov. Mike DeWine during his speech. "Do Something" became a citywide rallying cry, and state and local elected officials announced a yard sign campaign in October 2019—using those two words written in white on a black backdrop—to advocate for stronger gun laws.

Reynolds also had positive comments about the Dayton police and their actions that night, a fact he said surprised him considering he had been a past critic of law enforcement in general, particularly in relation to high-profile cases involving their actions against African Americans.

"The officers there wanted to help everybody," Reynolds said. "I'm glad they were able to react so quickly and took the shooter out."

Every mass shooting has its cycle. Grief, anger, calls for change. And too often, apathy. Americans have seen this happen in so many cities, so many venues and to so many different groups of people.

On Sunday, August 4, Anthony Reynolds wanted to have hope. Perhaps he was present that night—and survived—for a bigger purpose.

"Let's put human life before policy and party," he said. "I'm tired of hearing talking points. I'm speaking out because this is real. We need good police officers, good bystanders, good citizens. Everybody is capable of doing something."

Seven Days after the Dayton Shooting

FREDRICK MARION

Sometimes, you don't want to write anything.

The words gum up.

Who am I to talk about this tragedy?

I didn't lose anything.

I didn't lose anything compared to the people who lost their lives ... to the people who lost their siblings, mothers, fathers, daughters, sons ... to the people who had to run.

I didn't lose anything compared to the ones who knew the victims ... and the ones who saw them in the street.

I didn't lose a single thing that I can name.

But something's gone.

I've walked those cobblestones more times than I can count.

I was born in Dayton.

My will says I'll be buried here.

I want a pine coffin with no embalming fluid so the trees and grass and beetles can take back what they gave.

I've stumbled on that patio. I've eaten hot dogs in the street.

I bought coffee, books and a hat I never seem to wear.
I blew my cigarette smoke into the starry night.

One Halloween, I saw a girl flash the crowd from her second-story window, a plastic cup of beer spilling in her hand.

I've seen bands.

I've seen bridesmaids.

I saw a girl crying on a bench as the train went rumbling by.

You can take the person out of Dayton, but you can't take Dayton out of the person.

There's dirt under these nails.

There's a chin that's up when all the world looks like a fist.

My uncle passed away many years ago and someone said to me, "The strangest thing about losing someone is life keeps going on like nothing changed."

The trains are out there in the dark.

Their wheels are rolling — metal on metal — cutting Dayton right in half.

It doesn't matter how strong you are.

Even the strongman has his limits.

He tries to lift the weight, but it doesn't move.

It's the world that moves on without him.

In memory of Megan Betts, Monica Brickhouse, Nicholas P. Cumer, Derrick R. Fudge, Thomas J. McNichols, Lois L. Oglesby, Saeed Saleh, Logan Turner, and Beatrice N. Warren-Curtis.

This poem was originally published in Fredrick Marion's email newsletter.

Ode to Dayton

TIFFANY SHAW-DIAZ

you may have heard
about my city
splashed across headlines:

nine dead
dozens injured
from terror in the night

but you may not have heard
about the heroes
shielding others with their skin

and you may not have heard
about the peacemakers
singing in blood-covered streets

look beyond those headlines
and see the beauty
in our ashes

watch how quickly we rise
with golden wings
to soar into glorious light

All Together Now

AIMEE NOEL

The street-scrubbers from last night

are among the crowd, their hands still vibrating

with the feel of bristles on brick. Water pools

at the downslope of granite curbs though

Dayton has not seen rain in ten days.

The media tents camped on the sidewalk

force you into the crush of people

facing the vigil's stage. You move upstream.

Sometimes your shoulders are pulled

by the current opposing you. Because

in America you have the luxury of returning

to the closed street where nine people

were killed so early that morning you say *last night*,

because you still have the luxury of defiance,

the belief about lightning strikes and all that,

you are compelled to join hundreds to shout

at cardboard leaders from the capital city

who will cross the stage like two-dimensional

ducks. You will aim your grief at them

as scripted. Because the only thing different

about your trauma is the antique bricks

you stand on. Wax from vigil candles will seal

the names into stone. Candles doled out

from Kroger tote bags. Candles already

half-spent from tornadoes or the KKK protest

or maybe this tragedy was so hot the candles

burned themselves in anticipation of politicians

invoking God, which is to say, it's out of their hands.

And the release of doves. Because this is America

and we are nothing if not symbolic.

But before the singing of Cohen's "Hallelujah"—

which is about violence and sex after all

and how fitting, America?— you will drape

yourself over a stranger because in passing him

you recognize your own ashes and if you have

woven your bodies just right, both of his arms

under yours, you will let your knees soften.

If he pulls you closer, if you trust his ability

to hold your grief, if your cheek meets the soft part

of his chest, you will cry, open-mouthed,

stopping the flow of the crowd.

On a Sunday after the Shooting

JOEL PRUCE

"Deliver us serenity, Deliver us peace, deliver us loving;
We know we need it, You know we need it"
Heather and I got the kids and ourselves dressed and shuffled out the door on a bright blue morning. This was the first time our Jewish family went to church but it was a special occasion. Two days earlier, Kanye West was spotted with his family at the Cheesecake Factory. Rumors swirled and were then confirmed: he was bringing his Sunday Service revival from the deserted hills of Calabasas to Dayton, Ohio, a city recovering from a recent fit of mass violence.

Our location that morning was RiverScape—an adaptive public park that houses an ice rink during the winter, music festivals all summer, and regular Saturday morning community yoga. Pokemon Go zombies still pace adjacent to the fountains where diapered toddlers cool off. It's a wondrous spot overlooking the Great Miami River where kayakers paddle upstream as sunsets drop over their shoulders. In a deeply familiar place for city dwellers, reality TV stars appear through the looking glass. Kim and the kids are seated in a pen on the south end. Our host for the day, Dave Chappelle, saunters in with a subtle entourage, sipping coffee. It is Sunday morning, after all.

I thought for sure the word had gotten out but, as parishioners gather, the crowds remain thin. Some attendees take the church theme seriously donning their Sunday best, while many others remind the bespoke that on Sunday morning sweatpants are perfectly appropriate. We stand behind barricades waiting for something to happen, looking at a huddle of keyboards and drums under the apex of the tented area. On the north end, security shifts a section of fencing to begin to usher in musicians, elected officials, and families of the shooting victims. Once the first wave rings the instruments, everyone else is permitted to enter in loose concentric circles. As the first notes sound, there could not be more than two- or three-hundred people. Feels almost private and quite personal, but unsettling.

I couldn't shake the feeling that I had fallen prey to hype, the seduction of being in proximity to celebrity. Sunday Service possesses a unique allure of only existing for most in the disposable clips of an Instagram story. But here we were, uncertain about why: Was it for the chance at being captured in a viral social moment or to experience art firsthand? The non-reproducibility of a performance of this nature privileges the latter, but the former lurks. We thirst for novelty though are commonly treated only to sameness.

Somber spiritual key tones inaugurate "Ultralight Beam." The choir echoes its maestro, "This is a god dream/This is everything," and a shared energy tumbles through the air. The space between our heads and the two-story tent top contracts urging all of us to come together. Maybe it's Kanye summoning the divine. Maybe. Whatever it is, the vocal power under that tent steers it in and wraps me with it like one of those velour blankets from Target that sheds strange blue fur. It is tangible and soft on my skin. I want to run it back and forth through my thumb and forefinger. The crowd exhales as the first song ends and my nervous anticipation fades, replaced by a warm, calming confidence.

The set peaks for me with "Jesus Walks," a song that always fills this Jew with Christ envy. The baritone calls to a crew of slaves and chains clink. The chorus rises and the hyped crowd rocks back and forth like we are davening. And I'm not a religious man. When I was younger—twenty-five years ago—I knew that spirit. It wound and coursed through my body during song. But, my connection to that hysteria has since subsided and, in the intervening years, I've wondered what it means for an intimate relationship with emotional religiosity to vanish. Was it real at that time or imagined? I've felt other spirits since that time—of love, loss, fatherhood, and fulfillment—but not anything intersubjective among a group of strangers. I flashback to those earlier times and recall the corporeal sensation that accompanies faith; mind tricks played on the body. This moment feels fondly nostalgic yet entirely spontaneous and quite profound and it is only 10 a.m.

Since this performance, Kanye reprised Sunday Service on tour but Dayton was the first non-Calabasas, non-Coachella venue. And that felt special, like he was doing something singular for us, for our town, in our moment of despair. Our national surrogate and super-famous-but-it's-not-a-big-deal-when-you-see-him-at-the-grocery-store local, Dave Chappelle, made it all happen. It's what we needed.

"Are you ready for your blessings? Are you ready for your miracle?"

Gem City Shine, the massive and mysterious concert slated for that afternoon, was projected to welcome 25,000 holders of free but hard-to-get tickets back to the Oregon District. In the three weeks since the shooting that left nine bar patrons dead, Fifth Street became the site of impromptu memorials and temporary media encampments. Some businesses were open but others only so on ad hoc basis: Am I and my staff feeling well enough to provide customer service today? The shock of the shooting rippled up and down the block, traumatizing those likely to be out on a night like August 4 as well as those who call the District their home and/or place of business. The concert promised an opportunity for the greater Dayton community to reclaim the space, to replace mass violence with a cosmic smudge, a spiritual rinse, a pop culture enema.

Local and national observers spent the week speculating about the lineup of performers. As late as sound check, someone online swore they captured Lady Gaga behind a piano on the makeshift stage across from the Dublin Pub. An indecipherable photo even circulated of what must've been an enigmatic roadie because Gaga was not among us. Neither was Bradley Cooper, her *A Star is Born* co-star and Chappelle pal. John Legend, native son of Springfield, Ohio, never materialized. The Obamas didn't show up despite convincing accounts that Secret Service had scoured the area. Prince didn't come back from the dead to make us pancakes.

We were instead witnesses to an eclectic range of acts: Thundercat, multi-instrumental funk weirdo; mainstay Talib Kweli; Kanye acolyte Teyana Taylor; megastar Chance the Rapper; and hall-of-famer Stevie Wonder. Not bad for a market that can't typically attract artists away from Columbus or Cincinnati. Being graced with star power of this magnitude is a momentary departure from our position as a non-viable tour stop in an out-of-the-way pocket of the Midwest. Flyover country doesn't even adequately describe how overlooked Dayton is. We're not a place you struggle to care about from 30,000 feet. We're a place you pass on the highway, fully aware yet unmoved, as exit numbers cycle by.

This particular Sunday also marked Dave Chappelle's birthday. And, although Mayor Nan Whaley proclaimed the date "Dave Chappelle Day" in Dayton, the celebrity aura surrounding the lead-up receded to foreground the city. In between acts, Chappelle lifted us up and challenged us. Gem City Shine was as much a clever title as it was an imperative: Gem City, Shine! Chappelle was our cheerleader that day, urging us to emerge from a dark season with the brilliance of a rare stone. The shooting capped off a summer that began with a Ku Klux Klan rally, quickly followed by a series of devastating tornadoes. Dayton had the wind knocked out of its belly and we needed a dust-off and a pep talk: a serious heart-to-heart from someone who knew us and loved us. We were the guests of honor at someone else's birthday party.

It's a reactionary woke cliché by now to declare that "thoughts and prayers" are empty gestures for a nation bleeding out, particularly when they serve as the upper limits of effort that elected officials are willing to invest to ensure our public safety. However, loving prayers were extended to our city on Sunday as a balm to ease the trauma and tension of our summer. They rained down on the sweaty crowd as a sizzling relief, giving us all permission to feel good again.

"Just call out my name and you know wherever I am, I'll come running; You've got a friend"

Dave Chappelle does this shtick where his band or DJ rolls a familiar instrumental and he carols over it, leading the crowd in a rollicking singalong. James Taylor, for instance, or "Killing Me Softly With His Song." He doesn't have a good voice. It's rather raspy with hints of menthol but he can locate and sustain a melody. I've seen him do this previously at one of his famous Juke Joints—a barn party on a farm in Yellow Springs that runs late into the night and is likely to feature famous rappers, singers, or comedians. These events are never announced much in advance and tickets go quickly, but it's a true happening.

Both this Sunday's festival and the irregular pop-up parties are all the more meaningful in a city where things don't usually happen. Dayton is dull. If I had moved here in my twenties, I may have been bored. Now, in my late thirties, I'm the father of two and a partner to one and Dayton has all we need. Raucous entertainment or a thriving nightlife are not among them, but other things sustain my attention these days. Dayton's livelier now than when we first arrived eight years ago and trends are positive overall. Summers offer free concerts a few days a week at a venue paid for by a family philanthropy. These events provide a glimpse of what and who Dayton is: richly diverse, old and young, and desperate for reasons to come out of their homes and assemble together.

As the sets stretch on across this bright blue afternoon, a dank breeze of perspiration and weed smoke drifts through the crowd. Around me is a rare vision of our city: integrated, not segregated; hands in the air, not teeth clenched; joyful, not angsty. White people twerking to Lizzo beats. It was the happiest I've ever seen Dayton. No drama. No fights. No mean mugging. No day-drinking that turns a nasty corner when the sun sets. Wholesome entertainment. No raunch. No edge. No questionable content. Just love and positivity. Chappelle and his friends gave this city a hug when we needed one most.

We're a tough city accustomed to hardship, suffering through all the worst afflictions present across the country and throughout society. Dayton can be rough and ugly. Unconventionally beautiful would be a generous label and not wrong. Hardship is our ethos and the come-up is our calling card. Dayton is an underdog that draws on a legacy of innovation with its current sights set on the future, hoping to forget about the last fifty years of population loss, deepening segregation, and deindustrialization. Our history teaches us we've been great and our leaders coach us that we can revive that inventiveness for another go at greatness.

The summer of 2019 tested our resolve in entirely unanticipated ways. In the weeks after the shooting, people were raw. I saw bearded men cry in public and a persistent anxiety worn on the faces of strangers. And understandably so. Daytonians are a tough stock protected by a hard shell forged in the fire. #DaytonStrong became the hashtag because it has a better bounce than #DaytonSad or #DaytonVulnerable. On a Sunday after the shooting though, Dayton finally let its guard down.

Gem City Shine was a benefit concert, but not the conventional kind. Tickets were free and beer cost what beer costs. Buckets circulated to collect voluntary donations and a bunch of money was raised into a central fund for the families of shooting victims. So that's good, I guess. But it seems far beyond the point.

Usually a telethon or benefit concert features celebrities raising money from audience members for a distant, foreign, anonymous recipient: victims of famine or a hurricane. Not this time. No bloated Biafran children. No waist-deep flood waters. Just us, crowds of people sprawled across the intersection at Fifth and Wayne. The concert was for us. The beneficiaries were our neighbors and the space we inhabit together, briefly tainted by violence but not forever stained. The concert benefitted us by feeding our heart and airlifting us to higher ground. Just imagine if our concern for others in crisis revolved around raising their spirits first and raising money second.

On the Monday after the Sunday, we went back to work, bragging about what we'd seen but low-key about it. We knew how cool we were but promised to not let it go to our heads. Return to normalcy occurred by about noon but a lingering spiritual curiosity briefly buoyed my mood. Then the week moved on as weeks do and the glow wore off as glows do.

It turns out that living at a site of a mass shooting is not much different from watching it on television. Nobody knows what to do and everything feels wrong. Something about this, though, felt right.

"The Only This"

NICHOLAS HRKMAN

"Don't forget what this place is about," Dave Chappelle begged tens of thousands Daytonians from the massive stage he paid to build at the end of a street that, three weeks earlier, had been the scene of a mass shooting that killed nine and wounded twenty-seven more.

His event, "Gem City Shine," held on Sunday, August 25, was meant to raise money for the victims' families and to give the community a chance to reclaim a space that was taken from them. Bars and shops that once were overflowing on weekends had been struggling to bring people back in. The Oregon District, a cobblestoned stretch of bars, shops, and apartments, our city's place of power, possibility and acceptance, had been changed. No one was sure if it could ever be the same.

Before, on any given night, you might catch Dave Chappelle make an appearance on this street to drink or sing karaoke at one of the bars. He lives on a small farm a short drive from the city and appears so often and with so little fanfare that many of us simply know him as "Dave."

Don't forget what this place is about. Dave was talking about how mankind learned to fly in Dayton, Ohio, about how slaves fleeing the South found their freedom here. But memory is rarely so selective, and remembering is not a small request. I've talked to many who would like to forget.

"I should've stopped him, I saw him walking right there," my friend, a towering bartender, extends a massive hand toward the alley behind the patio where we were standing, the alley *he* took. His eyes are red and swollen.

"I can't fucking sleep, man," his voice shakes. "I keep seeing this girl's face, the blood. I ran out after I heard the shots. I tried to save her, but I knew she was already gone."

Someone nearby summons the rest of the patio to embrace him. A dozen strangers close around and share themselves with open arms.

I don't go to church. I'm not a particularly spiritual person, but Kanye West did not come to convert me. He came because he, like many other friends of Dave, was called to help people who were hurting. And so Kanye West quietly brought his Sunday Service to Dayton the morning of Gem City Shine to begin a day of healing.

Shamefully, I attended Sunday Service because I was curious. Because the tantalizing idea of being close to celebrity and fame does something strange to my mind. I did not go to heal or be healed, I went because I heard Kanye West might be at a small, urban park down the street from my apartment. We call the park "Dayton's front porch" because it is where we go to meet and greet each other at festivals and community events. As any proper Midwesterner would, I wanted to greet a guest on my front porch.

At nine in the morning, I approached the park's covered pavilion with only a few hundred other guests patiently waiting around the fenced perimeter. A white organ, drums and small stage had been placed in the middle. The families of victims were brought in first to gather around it, followed by members of local choirs and choirs flown in from LA. Finally, the eager crowd of the curious was allowed in behind them.

A pastor led the small gathering in worship, conducting the surrounding choir with hands waving and cutting through the electric anticipation in the air. With a downward gesture, he pushed the congregation low to the ground as he began to sing *hallelujah*. All joined, voices building up, up, up, singing *hallelujah* louder and faster as they rose. Jumping up and down, hundreds of hands reached skyward as if to pull something from above, greedy. The pastor sliced again and the chorus reaches its apex, a word repeated, screamed, a vessel filled with the joy and the grief of all those who breathed it into life again and again until the collected voices finally fell quiet.

"Turn to your neighbor and greet them!" The pastor said. "Find someone you do not know and thank them for their presence."

Wide smile met wide smile and strangers hugged one another. It was then I realized I had started to cry. Whatever was in that air, whatever we put into it or took from it—energy, electricity, community, God or otherwise—I needed it.

A drumline started to play and the choir joined them as cell phones raised above the crowd. Kanye West, wearing a navy shirt with "State of Ohio" printed in gold on his back, took the stage. The choir assumed a familiar chorus, his head nodding along with them before launching into the second verse of "Jesus Walks."

I know He hear me when my feet get weary and I see the piles of shoes found behind the bars, flung away as people scaled patio fences to escape.

The only thing that I pray is that my feet don't fail me now and I see the bloodied couple emerging from the Oregon District as I approached, saying there was a shooter at the bar where I was headed to meet a friend. Sirens and lights as police cruisers began to arrive from every direction. The police yelling for everyone to get back.

God show me the way because the Devil's tryna break me down and I'm on my phone trying to reach my friend. No response. Getting texts and calls from others. Calling again and again, texting others.

The only thing that I pray is that my feet don't fail me now and I'm running to his house blocks away. Pounding on the door. The breath I took when he and his girlfriend groggily approach and open it.

"What's wrong?"

A few days after the shooting, a reporter from New York joined some friends and I as we were drinking at a bar in the Oregon. She talked about how it feels to cover mass shootings, how painful it is to see the damage done to the communities.

"Is there anything different about us?" one of us asked.

She paused before answering: "No."

Almost desperately, I repeated the question. "Nothing? Anything you've seen here that feels different?"

"Honestly, no." She paused again. "You want your pain to be special, or different, but I've seen this before. Too many communities have this same pain."

I felt defeated. I wanted this stranger to see some unique resiliency about us, something distinctive born out of the recent experience of rebuilding after fourteen tornadoes ravaged the homes of my friends and neighbors, or of the grit in having protested against the KKK. I could feel it, a sense of forced anonymity, invisibility, of becoming numbered and not named. Nine dead, seventeen shot. There was another mass shooting across the country earlier that day—there would be another soon.

"You think it hurts now, with the constant media attention and not being left alone," she said. "But you don't want to be left alone. I've heard it's worse after we leave and the country moves on. You feel forgotten."

Forgotten, left behind, neglected, lost. After living in Dayton nearly my entire life, I've gotten used to hearing the city described in these terms. You start to feel them describe yourself. In truth, I have not always loved my city. My friends would tell you that I, after graduating college at the height of a recession and finding no job prospects in larger, more "exciting" places, dreaded the idea of going back. Why would someone want to live in a place the rest of the world has willfully forgotten?

In the last half-century, Dayton has lost nearly half of its peak population. Its longstanding industries abandoned their factories and headquarters. Most of those with the means fled the urban core for the suburbs and raised their children to believe the city was a dangerous place. Opioid addiction and despair tore through those that remained. Foreclosure, segregation, disinvestment, rust. In the ten years since I moved back after school, the city has shown promising signs of recovery, but we still have a steep hill to climb.

"When I'm out in LA, people always laugh at me and say, 'Dave, why do you live in Ohio?'" Dave said on stage as he kicked off the event. "You know what I tell them? 'Why the fuck not?'"

It's a joke, but it's an important non-answer that resonated with the crowd. We've all been met with the same question, posed by people from places that have not been forgotten. Dave goes on to mention the 250 other shootings this year, 250 other places that we will soon forget.

"But *this*," he points out to the crowd and beyond as he finishes. "*This* is the only *this*."

The beauty of that ineffable *this*. No, our pain is not unique. Our community grieves much like other communities grieve. But this is not Los Angeles and this is not New York. This isn't Toledo or Youngstown or Akron. This isn't Newtown, El Paso, or Parkland, either. This is unapologetically, incomparably Dayton. We don't have anything to prove to these other people and places. We have *this*.

At the end of Sunday Service, the pastor called Dave to the stage to speak.

"Today, the whole world is looking at you," Dave told us over the cheers.

I've talked to many who did not want to be seen after the shooting or the tornadoes, who did not want to be looked at by the world. They have not had time to grieve. They didn't want more outsiders looking in. Was this event coming too soon?

I'm sure some of them were right. But there was also an inescapable sense everywhere you went that something was still powerfully wrong. In the weeks after the shooting, small gestures of love and patience among strangers had become commonplace. Still, there was this sense of an open wound, of feeling weaker than we had before.

"We're still here." Dave continued. "We're still strong. The best way that we can honor our fallen is by getting up better than we were before."

And so, to help cleanse our wounds, he gave us his friends for the day. Chance the Rapper blessed us. Teyana Taylor, with her daughter in her arms, tearfully sang as images of the victims played behind her. Jon Stewart said we deserved to reclaim our space. Stevie Wonder reminded the crowd that someone loved us.

A city that has long struggled with loving itself faced a stage of stars that came to let the Gem City know it was not forgotten. At the end of the event, a rolling sea of cellphone lights shone on one man who loved us very much.

As tens of thousands of friends and neighbors made their way home, groups of volunteers formed to collect the litter left behind. On my way out, I saw a woman with a broken leg use her crutches to carefully, but with determination, push trash into piles for the volunteers to gather.

By morning, this place would be clean. Normal, even.

Originally published on Dayton.com, Sept. 25, 2019.

Holding Up the Sky

BRIDGET SHINGLETON HUTT

I cruise down Edwin C. Moses. Windows are down. Radio's off. It's a Wednesday night in early September. Starlings swoop around the stark skeleton of the Great Miami River bridge, and the sky is pinkly lilac in a way that makes me feel like I've fallen through a curtain and suddenly, somehow, found myself existing outside of time. Have always existed outside of time.

This land has been here forever. These rivers, their banks and rapids, curves and slopes. These skies. This soft, soft air.

Dayton hasn't always been ours, and it won't be forever. But for now it is. It is right now.

Right now I'm driving home from teaching my sophomores at UD. The windows are down, the radio's off, and Wednesday is the end of my teaching week, so I'm feeling pretty good. Class went well, and I'm tired and grateful.

A lot of things have been making me feel grateful these days. I'm grateful for getting to do work that I care about—to teach writing, to advocate for adult literacy, and to help organize one of Dayton's most vibrant annual events. I get to do these things with teams of passionate, compassionate people who challenge and inspire me. We care about each other. I never doubt it. I'm grateful for that too.

Dayton cares. Dayton cares a great deal about a great number of things, but more than anything, we care for each other.

Just over a month ago, nine people lost their lives in one horrific moment that shattered a beautiful Saturday night that, until that moment, was just like any other summer Saturday. Music played, beer poured, people danced, flirted, argued, smoked cigarettes. It should have been any old Saturday night, but it wasn't.

The next day was a blur. We came together. Friends poured downtown, refused to be afraid of or in the city we love. We ate and drank at bars and restaurants that opened their doors to us in our grief and confusion, that had pledged to donate proceeds to a tragedy fund that was still yet to be established.

This is part of what Dayton does. We give before we even know how. We take care of each other before asking who or why.

Dayton gave the world flight! We gave the world the cash register, the self-starting engine, and a flood plan. We gave the world the ice cube tray, for goodness' sake.

For goodness' sake, Dayton has given the world poets and humorists, actors and actresses, astronauts and leaders.

Dayton has always had a lot to give.

Dayton has not always been mine. Growing up in an Air Force family, I was always painfully jealous of people who had a hometown, who grew up in one place and knew it like the back of their hand. I never thought I would have that. I was wrong. I'm grateful for being wrong.

At some point it hit me that Dayton had become my home, though I couldn't tell you when. All I know now is that everything reminds me of here. Even things that are right here remind me of here. Two weeks ago I looked down at my flat-woven shoelaces as I stood near the stage at the Brightside during Dayton Music Fest. Paige Beller hypnotized the crowd, and I noticed my shoelaces, remembered weaving them flat so I wouldn't need to tie them earlier this summer at Springsfest. The music then connected me to the music before, to when I wove my shoelaces flat while sitting on a picnic blanket on a floor of pine needles that crunched every time we moved and that seemed to leave ancient scriptures pressed into our palms long after we sat up from leaning back too long, to stretch, to pay more attention to the music, the dogs napping nearby, or each other.

Everything here reminds me of here.

It's a Wednesday night in September. I'm driving home from class, and the sky is pink. I pull over for a moment, stop my car, remove the key from the ignition, get out, cross the street.

I remember this place. I remember it before tragedy arrived, and later I will remember right now.

Dayton is always changing. So am I, and so are we.

But right now, it's just a pink-sky Wednesday night. Traffic shushes by, mirroring the sweep of the river, without me. And I stand on the river bank with the starlings above, just another fixture on the hillside, holding up the sky.

I will remember this place.

Dayton, Strong

MAXWELL PATTON

We are the broken bone, snapped over and over again by unfortunate circumstances, that grows back each and every time sturdier than before.

We are the phoenix that rises from the ashes, ready to be born again after an inevitable demise.

We are Dayton strong.

Contributors

Ashley Bethard is a writer who lives in Dayton. Her essays, memoir, and short fiction have been published in *Catapult, The Rumpus, PANK Magazine, Hobart, Fanzine,* and others. She is a 2019 Tin House Winter Workshop alum in nonfiction, and was awarded the 2017 Ohioana Walter Rumsey Marvin Grant. She has an MFA from Ashland University.

Scot Brown is an associate professor of African American studies and history at the University of California, Los Angeles. Brown is the author of the book *Fighting For Us,* and has penned numerous articles on African American history, social/political movements, music and popular culture. He is a contributing author and the editor of the book, *Discourse on Africana Studies.* Brown is in the process of completing a book project exploring the city of Dayton as a 1970s musical hotbed of soul and funk bands. Brown has appeared as an expert commentator on African American music and popular culture for many programs on television, radio and social media: KLRU, National Public Radio, Sirius/XM Radio, DATV, BET/Centric, TV One, and VH1. Additionally, Brown has appeared in several documentaries on the civil rights and Black Power movements, including the PBS documentary *The Black Panthers: Vanguard of the Revolution.*

Annette Chavez is a family physician who has practiced in the Dayton area for the past 31 years. She is a graduate of the University of Dayton, the Ohio State University College of Medicine, and the St. Elizabeth Medical Center Family Practice Residency program in Dayton. Chavez is currently a solo independent physician at Carillon Family Practice in Kettering, Ohio. She has lived in the Dayton area for her entire life except for the four years in medical school in Columbus.

Mary Combs was born in St. Elizabeth's Hospital in Dayton in 1951. She spent her childhood in Belmont and Riverside. After graduating from the University of Dayton, where she met her husband Michael Bachmann, she received a degree in library science from Case Western University. As few library jobs were available in 1974, Combs ended up in information technology working for the Moyer Mortgage Company, and then as a contractor mostly on Air Force projects on and off Wright-Patterson Air Force Base. She recently retired.

Leah DeAloia is in the process of developing a collection of poems—of which "Mr. Davis Has Class" is one—with a working title *In the Heart of the Heart of the Heartland*, featuring contemporary artists of the Midwest. She is also editing her novel *Words to Die By*. Her fiction, poetry, and literary essays have won local and regional awards, and she has published fiction, essays, and book reviews in local newspapers and literary magazines. After stints in Ann Arbor, Michigan, and Honolulu, DeAloia returned to her hometown of Dayton, where she worked as a copywriter for several local ad agencies before accepting a position at the University of Dayton. For nearly two decades, she has been at UD teaching creative writing, rhetoric and composition, and literature courses.

Amanda Dee is a Chicago-based multimedia storyteller. She is the former editor-in-chief of *Dayton City Paper*, Dayton's alternative newsweekly. She is a writer for the arts publication and archiving initiative *Sixty Inches from Center*. Dee is also the associate producer of the oral history podcast *Moral Courage Radio: Ferguson Voices*, which documents voices from the Ferguson community in the wake of the 2014 police shooting of Michael Brown.

Terry Focht is a Dayton native. He has been married to his wife, Jan, for more than fifty-two years. They have one daughter, Terrill, and two cute, cuddly and crazy granddaughters, Natalie and Elena. They are now retired and living in Centerville, Ohio.

Joseph Gardner graduated from the University of Dayton in 2018 with a bachelor's degree in sport management, and researched UD basketball history for the article he wrote with his former professor, Peter Titlebaum. He is the assistant director of marketing—multimedia and design at Creighton University.

John Gorman was born and raised in Dayton and currently resides in Milwaukee. His work has appeared in numerous online outlets as well as in a couple small literary journals. He published an essay in Belt's *The Milwaukee Anthology*.

Nicholas Hrkman is a native Daytonian, a product of the Dayton Public Schools, a downtown resident, and a regular face around the Oregon District.

Betsy Hughes moved to Dayton from Philadelphia in 1964, when she and her husband started their thirty-year teaching careers both at newly formed educational institutions—he at the Dayton campus of Ohio State and Miami universities, soon to become Wright State University, and her at The Miami Valley School. Three collections of her sonnets were published in the last 10 years: *Breaking Weather*, winner of the Stevens Poetry Manuscript Competition (National Federation of State Poetry Societies Press, 2014); *Bird Notes* (Finishing Line Press, 2017); and *Forest Bathing* (Antrim House Books, 2019).

Oneita Jackson is a satirist, Detroit cab driver, and author of *Nappy-headed Negro Syndrome* and *Letters from Mrs. Grundy*. She earned an English degree from Howard University and was a copy editor for eleven years at the *Detroit Free Press*. During that time, she served as public editor, wrote music reviews, edited on the features, nation/world, and web desks, and received awards for her headlines. She also wrote the "O Street" column for three years; it received the newspaper's 2008 Columnist of the Year award. She stopped writing the column in May 2010 and returned to the news copy desk, where she stayed until August 2012. A native of Dayton, Jackson spent her summers in New York City and has lived in Washington, D.C., and Albany, New York.

Cynthia Ressler Keefer had a thirty-year career as an educator in Dayton Public Schools and is a graduate of the University of Dayton. She is the author of *Keys to the Cages*, a book about the 1930 Ohio penitentiary fire that changed America's penal system for the better. The book was written under the name Molly C. Cain.

Ron Knipfer is a retired engineer and United States Air Force officer. He worked at Sinclair Community College and Dayton RTA bus company after his retirement from the Air Force. He and his wife, Mary, have three children: Maureen, Ann, and John. He is in his 80s and enjoys golf, fitness training, and lifelong learning.

Shelley Kurtz Sommer graduated from Oakwood High School in 1979 and from the University of Dayton in 1983. She received her masters at the Center for the Study of Children's Literature at Simmons College in 2005. She is also the author of two biographies for young readers: *John F. Kennedy: His Life and Legacy* and *Hammerin' Hank Greenberg: Baseball Pio-*

neer. Hammerin' Hank Greenberg was named a 2012 Sydney Taylor Honor Book and a spring 2011 selection of the Junior Library Guild. She lives in Scituate, Massachusetts, where the people at her gym know she always wears a UD t-shirt!

Erica Manto-Paulson is a lifelong Ohioan and proud Daytonian who finds inspiration for her poetry in the fertile fields of her home state, drawing on a deep connection to the surrounding world and the "holy ordinary" of everyday life.

Fredrick Marion is working on his first novel, a fantasy book for young readers, with representation by The Bent Agency. His weekly emails go out to hundreds of writers and artists around Dayton and beyond. Learn more at www.fredrickmarion.com.

Michael McGovern spent more than a decade in Washington, D.C. and Columbus before finally making his way back to Dayton in 2019. He is the communications director with Innovation Ohio, a progressive think tank and advocacy organization. He has previously had communications and research roles with a variety of state and national advocacy organizations and campaigns. He lives in the Huffman Historic District with his wife and two cats.

Jesse Mullen lives in southwest Montana with his wife, children, four dogs, three horses and a mule. Since leaving the Dayton metro area in 2017, he purchased two small weekly newspapers and a bookstore. He misses Ohio a little.

Aimee Noel was displaced from the Rust Belt city of Buffalo, to another Rust Belt city in Dayton, where she lives with her wife in their 1890s home that requires as much attention as a relationship. She works as an educator and community activist. Currently, she is raising awareness about the food desert situation in the city and advocating for the integration of the visual and literary arts. Her work has been featured in *Provincetown Arts*, *Witness*, *Forklift, Ohio*, and elsewhere. She can also eat her weight in pierogi.

Maxwell Patton is an aspiring journalist and poet who loves to share facts and opinions through the medium of writing. He is a graduate of Sinclair Community College, and has earned his associates degree in multimedia journalism. Patton also performs regularly at the Dayton Poetry Slam.

Drew Perfilio is a concert industry professional living in Chicago, where he lives with his wife and his son. His Chicago credits include membership on a Mental Graffiti National Poetry Slam team and as an organizing member of the PolyRhythmic Arts Collective and Safe Smiles Open Mic. He was also an organizing member of the Dayton Poetry Slam in the early 'aughts.

Judd Plattenburg is a business owner in downtown Dayton, a photographer and an avid paddler. Judd was born and raised in Dayton and has stayed here to pursue his interests. When Judd is not running Oregon Printing Communications, he can often be found photographing, paddling (or both) along one of Dayton's beautiful rivers.

Joel R. Pruce teaches about human rights at the University of Dayton. He wrote a book called *The Mass Appeal of Human Rights* (2018) and leads the Moral Courage Project, a storytelling initiative that produces traveling exhibits, interactive websites, and a podcast series--all featuring first-hand accounts of frontline activists at domestic sites of human rights crisis, including Ferguson, El Paso, and Flint. Joel lives in the Historic South Park neighborhood of Dayton with his partner, Heather Atkinson, a political program director for the IUE-CWA labor union; their son and acclaimed toy musician, Wyatt; their evil genius daughter, Daisy; and their dog and in-house possum chaser, Teddy Bear.

Anthony Reynolds is a Dayton native and proud west Dayton resident.

Eric Rhodes was born in Akron: the erstwhile home of LeBron James, the Black Keys, and American rubber manufacturing. A transplant to Southwest Ohio, he earned his B.A. at Antioch College and his M.A. at Miami University. Eric is currently teaching history at the University of Angers in France. His writing has appeared in *Pieces of History*, *The Metropole*; *Origins: Current Events in Historical Perspective*, and *Tropics of Meta*.

Islom Shakhbandarov is a business and community leader in Old North Dayton and founder of the Ahiska Turkish American Community Center. He immigrated to the United States in 2004 as a refugee and moved to Dayton in 2007.

Tiffany Shaw-Diaz is a lifelong Dayton-area resident. She is an award-winning poet and visual artist. To learn more about her, please visit: www.tiffanyshawdiaz.com.

Bridget Shingleton Hutt is an adjunct instructor in the English department at the University of Dayton and the community engagement manager for the Brunner Literacy Center, an adult literacy center in northwest Dayton. Education and expression are her life's passions, as she is cognizant that all writing is an effort to connect, to share ideas with other people in other times and places. Dayton's history of creativity and innovation inspires her. She was a part of TEDxDayton in 2017 and has served TEDxDayton as a mentor to other speakers and performers and as a signature event co-chair.

Christy Lynne Trotter Simonson is a Dayton-area native. She currently teaches English composition at Sinclair Community College. She has published poetry in *Mock Turtle Zine* and short stories in *Flights*, Sinclair Community College's literary journal.

Hayley Snyder is an emerging writer who has been living in the Dayton area for about three years, and currently resides in Miamisburg. Throughout the week, she takes care of people's eyes as an ophthalmic technician. In the evenings and on weekends, she most likes to spend her time writing, drinking coffee, and chatting with a friend. A good session of Dungeons and Dragons is always welcome as well.

Ashley Stimpson is a writer based in Baltimore. Her freelance work has been published or is forthcoming in *Longreads, Atlas Obscura, Johns Hopkins Magazine, Belt, Blue Ridge Outdoors* and elsewhere. Her literary nonfiction has been nominated for a Pushcart Prize and published in *Entropy, Camas, Cagibi*, Brevity's Nonfiction Blog, and elsewhere.

Jill Summerville is an Ohio Arts Council Individual Artists With Disabilities grant recipient for 2020. Though her PhD is in theater, she primarily works as a freelance writer and editor. Her work has appeared in *Mental Shoes, Onstage Blog, Dayton City Paper, The Yellow Springs News, Amplify The Spirit* (2020 book release) and *The Washington Post*. She may be writing a love letter for you right now.

Donna Sword is a native Daytonian, freelance writer, history enthusiast, and lover of all things dog. She lives in a small town in northwestern Montgomery County with her husband, two dogs, and a ridiculously adorable puppy she's raising to be a service dog for the non-profit Canine Companions for Independence. She shares her stories on volunteer puppy raising at Raising a Super Dog (www.rasuperdog.com) and has a local history blog at House BlackSword (www.houseblacksword.com).

Matthew L Szozda is an educator, artist, writer, and creative advocate from Dayton. He currently teaches art and design to young children in the Dayton area. In 2019, Szozda was selected as the Ohio District 3 Teacher of the Year. He uses this platform to promote purpose-based learning across Ohio.

Bob Taft teaches at the University of Dayton. He is a former governor of Ohio.

Peter Titlebaum is a professor at the University of Dayton. His areas of expertise include marketing, sales, fundraising, activation, return on investment and return-on-objective strategies. He is a frequent speaker with more than 200 presentations and 150 publications to his credit.

Bill Vernon studied English literature, then taught it mostly at Sinclair College, but also with brief stints at UD and Wilberforce University. Writing is his therapy, along with exercising outdoors and doing international folk dances. Five Star Mysteries published his novel *Old Town* in 2005, and his poems, stories and nonfiction have appeared in many magazines and anthologies.

Nan Whaley is proud to choose Dayton as her home. Originally from Indiana, Whaley attended the University of Dayton, where she graduated in 1998, and soon settled in the Five Oaks neighborhood where she and her husband, Sam, reside today. First elected to the Dayton City Commission in 2005, she was the youngest woman ever chosen for a commission seat. She was proud to be elected as Dayton's mayor in 2013 by a double-digit majority. As mayor, she has focused on the areas of community development, manufacturing, and women and children.

Merle Wilberding lives in the City of Dayton's Rubicon Mill development. He has practiced law for more than fifty years, and has been at the law firm of Coolidge, Wall Co. LPA, since 1973. He has written a book on the history of the Coolidge law firm, *150 Years of Cool Law*, as well as five other books. He is a regular op-ed contributor to the *Dayton Daily News* (approximately one column per month for more than the past five years). A Vietnam War veteran, he served in the U.S. Army as a member of the JAG Corps and was recently inducted into the Ohio Veterans Hall of Fame.

Herbert Woodward Martin was born in Birmingham, Alabama, on October 4, 1933, to David Nathaniel and Willie Mae Woodward Martin. When he was twelve years old, he moved with his mother to Toledo, Ohio, where he graduated from Scott High School. He began his studies at the University of Toledo. He continued them at SUNY at Buffalo, then at Middlebury College, and finished at Carnegie Mellon University. He came to the University of Dayton in the fall of 1970, where he currently serves as professor emeritus. He is nationally known as a Dunbar scholar for his readings of the poetry of Paul Lawrence Dunbar.

Belinda Wright is a finance program manager for Qbase LLC, a provider of data products and services. She is also a house manager with the Victoria Theatre Association. Wright enjoys writing, reading, attending live theater productions, and traveling to quiet, out-of-the-way destinations for reflection and relaxation.